NO LIFE OF MY OWN

Frank Chikane

NO LIFE OF MY OWN

An Autobiography

Frank Chikane

WIPF & STOCK · Eugene, Oregon

Wipf and Stock Publishers
199 W 8th Ave, Suite 3
Eugene, OR 97401

No Life of My Own
An Autobiography
By Chikane, Frank
Copyright©1988 Orbis Books
ISBN 13: 978-1-60899-287-4
Publication date 11/30/2009
Previously published by Orbis Books, 1988

Contents

v

Acronyms

ANC	African National Congress
AZAPO	Azanian People's Organization
BCM	Black Consciousness Movement
BPC	Black People's Convention
CCFD	Comité Catholique Contra la Faim pour le Développement
EAAT	Ecumenical Association of African Theologians
EAATSA	Ecumenical Association of African Theologians in Southern Africa
EATWOT	Ecumenical Association of Third World Theologians
ICT	Institute for Contextual Theology
IYCC	Interdenominational Youth Christian Club
KRO	Krugerdorp Residents Organization
MUCCOR	Ministers United for Christian Co-responsibility
NUM	National Union of Mineworkers
NUSAS	National Union of South African Students
PAC	Pan African Congress
SACC	South African Council of Churches
SACP	South African Communist Party
SACTU	South African Congress of Trade Unions
SASO	South African Student Organization
SCA	Soweto Civic Association
SCM	Student Christian Movement
SRC	Student Representative Council
UDF	United Democratic Front
UNISA	University of South Africa
WCC	World Council of Churches

Foreword

This is more than an autobiography. It is an excellent example of what theologians now call "narrative theology." There is so much about the meaning of Christian faith that can only be expressed in narrative form. Biblical revelation itself comes to us largely in the form of stories, histories, parables, and biographies. Among the various forms of narrative theology the autobiography has a special place. It is a kind of narrative confession of faith. Frank Chikane's autobiography is the confession of faith of a man of great faith who has learned to understand the meaning of this faith in the crucible of apartheid South Africa.

I first met Frank when he was a young minister in the township of Kagiso. Later I worked with him in the Institute for Contextual Theology. At that stage he did not have much in the way of academic theological qualifications, although he never ceased to read and study theology. What he had in abundance, however, was an instinct for theology. He had, and still has, an extraordinary ability to articulate the practical meaning of faith in the context of our South African crisis, suffering, and conflict. It is a theological ability that arises out of the experience of a tried and tested faith—as his autobiography makes abundantly clear.

Frank is a living example of what we mean by contextual theology. He was, more than anyone else, the inspiration and driving force behind the Institute for Contextual Theology and the Kairos Document. The Institute is a facilitating body that enables people to do their own theology from within their own contexts. The Kairos Document was a joint effort by numerous Christians giving expression to their understanding of faith at that particular moment. Frank's role (together with others) was to enable people to articulate what they really believed. He is, in the very best sense of the word, a born leader.

After this book was completed, Frank's ability as a leader reached its fullest acknowledgement to date. He was elected Secretary General of the South African Council of Churches (SACC). Not only was he the youngest person ever elected to this very influential position; he was also the only person to reach that position without climbing the ladder of leadership in his own church. In fact, his own church, the Apostolic Faith Mission, is not a member church of the SACC. As he tells us at some length in his book, much of Frank's struggle to be a Christian was a painful struggle with the leadership of his own church.

Today in South Africa Frank Chikane exercises a quiet but powerful leadership that is inspired by ''the Son of Man who came not to be served but to serve and to give his life as a ransom for many'' (Mk 10:45). As the title of his book indicates, Frank has indeed no life of his own. He has given his life and is still giving it, for the people of South Africa.

ALBERT NOLAN
Johannesburg

Preface

For all of us life is a story of liberation and enslavement. But we in South Africa experience this reality in an intense and acute form. Our pilgrimage as Christians has taken us through a moral, spiritual and political battleground and into a liberation struggle. It has not been an easy journey, and we are not yet at our destination.

For almost a year, from 1986 to 1987, I lived the life of a fugitive and learned at first hand the experience of countless others of my fellow countrymen and women. Part of this time I spent hiding in South Africa, part of it abroad. During it, I had time to reflect on my life and make the agonizing decisions demanded by the crisis in South Africa. This book was part of this process. I felt that my spiritual journey, far from being unique, was being traveled by many young Christians today. I wanted to share my thoughts and my experiences with them. I had little idea that within a few months my life would be changed dramatically by my appointment as general secretary of the South African Council of Churches.

My life has changed in several ways since that time, but the lives of my fellow countrymen and women have not. I hope that this book may help them make some sense of the journey that Christians are making today under apartheid and help my fellow pilgrims on their way to our common liberation.

Above all I hope it will help all those who face the dilemmas of being Christian in this evil apartheid society and who, because of their commitment to the liberation struggle, can truly say they have no life of their own.

In the past few years, friends here and abroad have been encouraging me to put in writing my experiences during my ministry in a conflict-ridden society. Their motivation was that my experiences can help and enrich other people who are going through similar experiences here at home and in other parts of the world.

But it was John Pobee of the Unit of Theology and Education of the World Council of Churches (WCC) who finally convinced me to work on the book. I made use of the time when I was in "hiding" (underground) in South Africa to prepare the material. I wish to thank all these friends, particularly John Pobee, for encouraging me to produce this manuscript.

A friend who needs to be given credit for this book is Ian Linden of the Catholic Institute for International Relations, who accepted my request to edit all the scripts I produced. His willingness to bend his schedule to give this book priority is highly appreciated.

I need also to thank the Institute for Contextual Theology (ICT) for offering to sponsor this project and the ICT staff, particularly Mrs. Esther Sentshomedi, for collecting all my documents and letters and for typing the manuscript. My thanks go also to Skotaville Publishers, particularly Mr. Mothobi Motloatse, for offering to publish this book and for putting pressure on me to work on the manuscript.

Above all I wish to thank my wife, Kagiso, our children, Obakeng and Otlile, for their patience, encouragement and support during all these experiences. I am what I am because of the type of partner I have in this ministry.

FRANK CHIKANE

INTRODUCTION

A Letter to All Who Care

In 1986 I was forced to go into hiding in South Africa. It had become apparent from the frequent visits of the security police to my house and workplace that I had reached the top of the list for arrest. I stayed in hiding for several months. It is not easy to avoid arrest and, as the weeks passed, the pressure mounted. I had a number of near escapes and, by the law of averages, it was only a matter of time. Training as a pastor does not equip you for the life of a fugitive.

I slipped abroad to Europe to attempt to take an examination as an external student of UNISA (University of South Africa). This proved impossible, however, as the university authorities insisted I take the exam in a South African embassy or consulate. I also planned to visit friends and partners and share with them our pains and sufferings in South Africa. Many friends wanted me to stay abroad and felt that any return to South Africa would be suicidal. And what my friends were saying to me made a lot of sense. It was an agonizing period of exile, and during it I learned what other exiles have to suffer.

One thought dominated my mind: my congregation, friends and comrades in Soweto and around South Africa did not have my luxury of indecision. They had to stay and face the music. How could I abandon them? How could I explain to them why the demands of the struggle dictated that I stay in exile? I could not gather them together and explain all the reasons for staying.

So I decided to go home. I felt that I owed it to all who had wanted to hold me back out of love to write to them and explain.

The letter that I wrote to them, fully expecting the worst on my return, follows. It makes a good start to the longer explanation that follows of my longer pilgrimage as a Christian under apartheid.

---

12 March 1987

To all those who care, to friends, brothers and sisters in the Lord, and to the Church of Christ at large:

The decision has been made, and I am on my way into that beleaguered country, South Africa. I have made the decision being very much aware of the consequences thereof: the possibility of being detained and imprisoned for long periods of time without any charge; the possibility of being tortured again, like many of my fellow sisters and brothers at home; the possibility of being eliminated or assassinated by agents of the apartheid regime, as they have already done with some of my dear brothers and sisters who committed themselves to the noble goal of a just, nonracial, democratic and peaceful society, and to the ideal of the kingdom of God in this world.

But why make this type of decision? To this question I must answer that I cannot explain in reasonable terms the decision I have made. When challenged by well-meaning friends who were concerned about my life, my well-being and the safety of my family (Kagiso, my dear wife and our two boys: Obakeng [6] and Otlile [2½], who have never been given a chance to make their choices), I simply crumbled. My action looks senseless, futile, suicidal, inconsiderate, stupid, and one can continue endlessly with these descriptive words that characterize my state of affairs. In short, I can't defend this position.

But why have I moved against the tide of reason? The cries of my people at home, the call of those who are in distress, who live between life and death on a daily basis; those who are in the heat of things, who have no other options but to face the guns of the apartheid security forces; the call of those who have left their families and have been in hiding or underground for the last nine months since the state of emergency—and these are in the thousands; the call of women, men and children in Soweto who believe that my presence, in terms of my ministry, will make a difference; this is the call that sends me back home.

The question is, given the State of Emergency and the closure of all possible nonviolent and peaceful forms of intervention; given that some of us have just "qualified" by proclamation to go to prison, and most probably would be whisked away or eliminated— should we make an appearance, let alone an intervention? What role does one have there? What am I called to come and do? Am I being called just to go to prison or die? Is that the intention of those who have sent the distress message to me?

No, I do not believe that this is their intention. I don't even believe that this seemingly logical end is in their minds. I believe that the enormity of the situation, their life-and-death situation, looms high over and above this rational consideration, and I understand this. Rather than focus on this seemingly irrational call, I have been overwhelmed by the very need that supersedes any rational consideration. I cannot therefore explain what I am doing except that I am going to be present with them, in life or death. I believe that it is the presence, even if it is a powerless form of presence, that they are crying for. I am going there just to be present.

Throughout this painful and agonizing experience, for the last few months, I have begun to see the story of the Passion in a new light. This experience has opened my eyes to a new and deeper reality about the gospel of the Cross. It has become clearer to me than ever before that Jesus in fact did not want to go to the Cross. He willed that the cup could pass him (Matthew 26:36–46); he wished that the cup could be removed from him (Luke 22:39–46); but he had to give in to the will of his Father.

No one really wants to go to the Cross, or the *way* of the Cross, but it has dawned on me in a new way that it does not look as if we can achieve our liberation in South Africa without going through the Cross. Given the determination of the white, racist, minority regime to defend and maintain the unjust privileges of this 15 percent of our population, even at the expense of the lives of the black 85 percent; given that most of the western superpowers are seemingly not persuaded by moral or just considerations over and above their economic and national security interests, and thus are determined to side with the apartheid regime; it does not look as if we can reach this vision of the *basileia* without going through the Cross. It looks as if it is in our death that we shall rise again into a new and just society. It looks as if it is in our weakness that we become strong; in our powerlessness in the face of the powerful odds that we shall gain power—the people's power, God's power—and through this seemingly hopeless situation there can be hope to free or liberate the oppressors and those who are intoxicated with power.

The second shock in my life throughout this period was that, although I had understood the message of taking sides with the poor, the oppressed, the weak—that is, the victims of society—following in the steps of the Lord, it did not occur to me that I would be required to go the whole way through. Even if I may theoretically have been aware of this possibility, it never occurred to me that I would have to go through it all myself, through it all with the people. Yes, I am scared about this reality. I wish I could avoid it, let it pass me, pass to others, so that I could live a normal life like other people. I am scared that if this is the will of the Lord, I will not escape it. I cannot hide myself from the Lord. In the midst of all this, in this struggle I have with the Lord, I pray that if I have to go through it all, it must be only with the Lord!

There are two stories in the Bible that loomed in my mind as I meditated on this issue: the story of Jesus' journey to Jerusalem that reached its climax on the Cross, and the story of Paul's journey, also to Jerusalem, which ended up with him in prison. Apartheid South Africa is indeed a Jerusalem of our time. When Jesus drew near and saw the city of Jerusalem he "wept over it," saying, "Would that even today you knew the things that make for peace! But now they are hid from your eyes. For the days shall come upon you when your enemies will cast up a bank about you and surround you, and hem you in on every side, and dash you to the ground, you and your children within you, and they will not leave one stone upon another in you, because you did not know the time of your visitation" (Luke 19:41–44).

This is the Kairos. It is our Kairos and I beg you, sisters and brothers, to pray with us, to act with us, even if it might cost us pain, to help us deliver this new baby—the new, just, democratic and nonracial South Africa where all will live in peace. In particular I ask you to pray with me for my family, about which I feel guilty, because my decision puts them in danger and deprives them of a normal family life.

I am now halfway to Jerusalem, and maybe I should put down my pen with only one promise: if I am not kept in chains, I shall keep our communication line open.

Sincerely yours,
Frank Chikane

NO LIFE OF MY OWN

My Early Days: Schooling in a "White Man's Country"

But what about my parental family? I do not believe that about thirty-seven years ago, when my father, James, and my mother, Erenia, brought me into the world, they knew what the future held in store. Maybe if they knew they would have decided not to bring me into this world. I was born against all odds. After their first child was stillborn, with my mother almost left for dead, the medical profession warned her not to try another baby. Belonging to a traditional African society where a woman with no children was simply no woman, she ignored the warning, and my brother, Rodgers, was born in 1948. I followed him on January 3, 1951. And I was followed by Walter in 1953, Abie in 1957, Thabile in 1962, Dorcas in 1964, Patricia in 1966, and Khotso in 1969.

Of course my mother did not see most of her children after delivery because she became unconscious, most of the time for days, and was kept at the hospital at times for months, before coming back home to be with the new baby. What an oppressive society for women. But, anyway, I was born.

I have mentioned my date of birth but I have not said where I was born. If you are black in South Africa, and of my generation, you cannot be sure of your actual place of birth because what you are told is likely not to be true. Because of the Influx Control laws of South Africa, where you are born can determine your whole future and can even separate you from your parents. For instance, had I been born in Bushbuckridge in the Eastern Transvaal where our grandparents are, I would not have the right to work or own a house in Soweto, Johannesburg. Inevitably my parents would claim

1

that I was born in Johannesburg, in Soweto. In some instances, even if a family was just traveling or visiting, they had to make sure that the mother was in the right place, for the sake of the child's future. No one in such a system can afford emergencies (babies who come before their time.) So I am said to have been born in Johannesburg, at No. 7 Orlando East. No birth certificates existed in those days. Anyway, babies were delivered at home with the help of older experienced women in the extended family. The truth may come out after our liberation but now it is a State of Emergency, and no truth can be uttered!

Our mother was weak, given the way she had to give birth, and had a heart condition. For this reason she stayed most of the time in Bushbuckridge, where our grandparents lived, away from the fast and chaotic ghetto life of Soweto. Thus during our early life we used to stay with her—maybe she was brought to Johannesburg to give birth to us, and then returned to Bushbuckridge afterwards. But once we qualified to go to school, we were taken away from our mother to stay with our father at No. 869 Tladi, Soweto, where my father had had a house since 1957. He still lives there with my mother and the other children who have not yet become independent or have not found alternative accommodation, scarce as it is for blacks in South Africa. If we had started school in Bushbuckridge, we would not have been allowed to get a passbook that gave us rights to live and work in Soweto.

So we started cooking and doing our own washing at the age of about nine years or so. I remember vividly that our black school trousers were covered with iron marks because we burned them while pressing them. And if I cooked "pap" and it spoiled, I would quickly empty the pot into the garbage, clean the pot before my dad noticed, and start again. I had my primary education at Hlolohelo Primary School, then from 1963 to 1966 I attended Tau Pedi Higher Primary School. Our mother joined us more permanently from 1962–1963 because she could not stand living away from her children any longer.

My father initially wanted me to be a lawyer, and he encouraged me as early as elementary school to begin to think about it. But during my secondary school education at Naledi High School (which was then called Soweto Secondary School), I felt more at home with mathematics than with any other subject. A black child excelling in mathematics! What would you do in our crazy country? Verwoerd had already provided an answer as early as 1948, when he warned those "engaged in seeking learning . . . which they use to cross the border line of European life . . . I want to state here unequivocally now," he said, "the attitude of this side of the House that South Africa is a white man's country and that he must remain the master here." On another occasion he said: "There is no place for him (the Bantu) in the European community above the level of certain forms of labour. Until now he has been subjected to a school system which . . . misled him by showing him green pastures of European society which he was not allowed to graze." He said: "What is the use of teaching the Bantu child mathematics when it cannot use it . . .?" This is the origin of the Bantu education system that blacks have rejected. It was made law in 1953.

After my pass with distinction at Secondary Certificate level, undeterred by Verwoerd's racist utterances, I was encouraged to go into the medical field. I proceeded to Orlando High School, where Mr. T. W. Kambule was principal. He became my mathematics teacher for two years, and during the last year I registered with two other students to do what was called additional mathematics. During these two high school years, I became more interested in becoming a mathematician or a mathematical physicist than a medical doctor.

This is what I tried to do at the University of the North in Pietersburg, one of the bush universities created exclusively for blacks after the 1959 University Extension Act. This act in effect barred joint and equal university training for blacks and whites, and confined blacks to these bush universities (they were called bush universities because they were built very far from the cities, which were declared white areas in accordance with the apartheid laws). My majors here were applied mathematics and physics.

Like many other black students, I was forced to terminate my studies right at the end of the BS degree after a lot of students were detained following what is now known as the "FRELIMO Rally," when we celebrated the liberation of Mozambique in 1974. What struck me then as a student was the fact that some groups of people, mostly Portuguese origin, held a protest on this day against the liberation of Mozambique, and they were not interfered with, while we were attacked by the police for celebrating the very same occasion. During this time, with most of the Student Representative Council members in detention, on the run, or in exile, I participated in the leadership of the student body when I was elected to head a students' legal aid fund with Ishmael Mkhabela and Griffiths Zabala as joint trustees. We took responsibility for the welfare of the detained students, of their families, and of the student body.

It was at this stage that my parents realized I was on a deadly dangerous route. They became more concerned about my safety and my future. When I gave evidence to the Snyman Commission, appointed to investigate the source of the September 24, 1974, unrest on campus, it became clear that I had come to the end of my career at that university. I had given evidence against the university and the police, and therefore against the state. At one time during this crisis, when I was making regular trips between Pietersburg and Johannesburg to get lawyers for the detained students and make contact with their families, my mother asked me why I was busy endangering myself instead of sitting in the university and completing my degree. I do not like my reply to this question because it seems quite arrogant today. I said to her: "Suppose I was in prison and Cyril Ramaphosa was visiting you to brief you about my position, like I am doing. Would you say the same to him?" (Cyril Ramaphosa, now general secretary of the National Union of Mineworkers, was among the detained students, and I used his name because my mother knew him.) Of course she broke down and said to me, "Remember that you are my child."

The problem is, everyone is someone's child. My experience of the last few years has taught me that it is good to read about brave men and women in history, people who have sacrificed their lives for others: the Mandelas, the Sisulus, the Bikos, the Peters, Pauls and Johns . . . and Jesus himself. These are people of historic importance who are worthy to be praised, who deserve to be called heroes and martyrs. But no one wants to be in their shoes or to go through the same experiences.

It is difficult to think of the twenty-five years that Mandela has spent in prison. During one of my detentions I converted his time in prison into days and compared it with the time I had spent in detention, and then I realized that my pain was negligible compared to the pain that Mandela was going through. He is also a human being. He also has children and a wife he has not stayed with for all these years. He is also someone's child. He also wants to live a normal life like others. In one of his writings he talked about being underground and the pain of leaving his family, his wife and children, of leaving home, of abandoning his legal practice, all for the noble goal of justice in South Africa.

The question is, whose child should it be? Whose wife? Whose husband? Whose mother? Whose father?

How was my BS degree terminated? While we were rejoicing, singing solidarity songs and chanting slogans like "Viva FRE-LIMO," "Viva Machel," "Freedom in our lifetime," "*A luta continua,*" the police descended on the campus and ordered us to disperse because, we were told, the meeting was unlawful. Although frustrated and disappointed, we left the hall singing *"Nkosi Sikelel' i-Afrika,"* the national anthem, which signified that we were closing the meeting. We were then attacked by the police with dogs, sjamboks and tear gas, and a lot of students were badly injured. That night most of the SRC members were detained. Being elected as the students' detainee-and-legal-aid-fund trustees, we assumed the leadership of the student body with the remaining members of the SRC.

Faced with this crisis, the student body decided on a sit-in that lasted for six days in protest against what they saw as an unwarranted and violent attack on them, and in solidarity with the detained student leaders. The sit-in ended eight days before my final examinations. The pressure of the sit-in, the problems of students with the lecturers (who were mostly conservative Afrikaners) as they tried to go back to class, the responsibility for the detained students, coupled with preparations for giving evidence to the Snyman Commission, were too much for me, added to my preparations for the examination. I had a mental breakdown in the middle of the examination, and the university sent me out of one of the examinations to Pietersburg hospital. When I applied, with all the medical certificates, for an *aegrotat,* the university refused one.

The following year I went back to the university to complete the degree, but one of the sympathetic black lecturers advised me not to try because it was clear that I was going to be victimized. Although I had done all the work for the degree, I had been ground down, and the knowledge remained "noncertificated."

Our African Spirituality:
Learning to Be Christian
at the Grass-roots

I was born into a Christian family, especially on my maternal side.
At the beginning, my father was not such an enthusiastic Christian
as my mother, but in the 1960s regular family prayer meetings developed into prayer meetings for people from the surrounding area.
A house church started in our home, and later it was accorded the
status of a branch assembly of our church, the Apostolic Faith Mission. As the membership grew, the house became too small and a
school classroom was rented. As this congregation grew, my father
was encouraged to train as a pastor, and, in 1975, he took over the
congregation as its pastor until today. They have since built a church
in Naledi, Soweto.

Growing up in this type of environment, I participated in the
development of this grass-roots congregation and, around 1968, at
the age of eighteen, I had already become secretary of the congregation and served on their assembly board (the parish council). But
my involvement in the church had started as early as eight years
old. I was left with my grandmother and worshiped with her. One
day I was asked to preach to the congregation on a Sunday morning. I do not remember why they chose me to do so at that age,
but nevertheless they did. I remember my grandmother going through
John 14 with me in preparation for the sermon. Because I was so
young and short, I was made to climb on a chair to deliver that
sermon. I do not remember whether I really preached a sermon or
whether I just repeated John's record of Jesus' words. I suspect that
this text was picked up because it was, and still is, a famous text

in funerals and night vigils, and would have been well-known to me. This was my first sermon.

Our church is a classical Pentecostal church, where small congregations start mostly in houses and in some instances under trees in rural areas. Services of worship are participatory. People sing together, share their individual experiences during the week, and pray with and for those who are sick. The pastor, elder or deacon selects a text, preaches on it and then lets as many members of the congregation as possible express their views about the text or respond to it. Given this context, you begin participating in the congregation very early in life. During the latter part of the 1960s, my brother and I teamed up with our parents to conduct evangelistic missions as far afield as Witbank and in the Bushbuckridge area.

During this time there was a lot of ecumenical activity, not necessarily sanctioned by the official churches, between people of different churches. I believe that this ecumenical dimension was made possible by our traditional communal African life, where all families within the same locality share together in their pain, suffering and successes, supporting one another and sharing in a common struggle for survival. During evening services—particularly Wednesdays and Fridays and weekend "wake" *(Umlindelelo/ Moletelo)* services—Catholics and Protestants, traditional mission churches, evangelical Pentecostal churches and African independent churches of the Ethiopian, apostolic and Zionist kinds, worshiped together and supported one another. If one church had a building project, all were invited to make a contribution during an all-night service. The same was done if anyone had to travel a long distance to see his or her family, was separated by the migrant labor system, if a person's contract was over or terminated, or if a pastor was moved from one place to another. The same also occurred if a tragedy struck a particular family or community, if someone had passed away, was disabled, unemployed, sick, and so on, or if a fire or lightning struck.

These days you still find a lot of this type of activity among the African independent churches in South Africa. In sociological terms, this is a typical working-class survival strategy. Both Pentecostal and Zionist churches are known to thrive in working-class circles among the poorest and most oppressed sectors of any society in

Africa, Asia or Latin America. Research shows that the growth of the Pentecostal movement in the United States in the last century broke out among these classes of people. The participation of black members of the traditional mission churches in this grass-roots ecumenical activity is a sign of the class contradictions within these churches, which leave most of the needs of the working-class membership (about 80 percent of their total membership) not met. Although some work has already been done on this area of the class dimension of the Pentecostal and indigenous grass-roots churches in most Third World countries, further analysis and research is needed to explain this phenomenon and put it on the agenda of the universal Church.

This is the context in which my faith developed. Our spirituality was a holistic form of spirituality, with no differentiation between the spiritual and the social. Our services of worship, our spiritual activism, were launched within the very social dynamics of our society. In any case, the African worldview of life and its conception of some form of deity were never dualistic. Africans' total life experiences were understood and interpreted in relation to their God. If a tragedy happens in a family, God must be involved—negatively or positively. If someone is unemployed or dismissed from work, God must be involved. If an accident happens to a person, God must be involved. For the African, God cannot just be a spectator in the war that is raging between the evil spirits and the spirit of righteousness, between God and the devil. You may call it a struggle between justice and injustice, between the oppressors and the oppressed, and some might express this dialectic as that of class struggle.

Whichever way you think about it, this is how grass-roots Africans in South Africa have always visualized and understood their spirituality. To them, God cannot be aloof in and throughout this course of suffering, pain and death, whether caused by natural forces or by human systems and structures. God must be involved to produce goodness in it. They go through these struggles looking forward to the day when Jesus will come again for the second time to destroy this evil world and replace it with a new earth and a new heaven, where their tears will be wiped away, where death shall be no more, nor shall there be any more pain. This was our vision of the kingdom, and all looked forward to that day.

But in hindsight—and through my interaction with African independent churches and my involvement with the Institute for Contextual Theology—I realize that while this grass-roots form of holistic spirituality addressed our spiritual and social needs, it did not address the source of this country's social abnormalities. It was more of a survival strategy than a strategy to end the victimization. I say this, being aware that some of the African independent churches have attempted to address the victimizer: as in the Bambata rebellion in 1906 and the Bullhoek massacre of 1921.* These were isolated events, though, which cannot be said to form the major thrust of this African spirituality. The missing link here was a direct confrontation between evil and goodness in the world, and this will be the subject of the following section.

*The rebellion against the poll tax led by Chief Bambata in Natal and the Bullhoek land occupation in the Eastern Cape both began in movements of independent churches. In both cases the police and army reacted violently, causing great loss of life. (Ed.)

Escaping the God of the Oppressor: Finding My Faith

Although holistic in its context, the limited form of spirituality that I grew up with raised questions for me during my secondary school education. The contradictions within our society, an exploitative, apartheid society, became clearer as my consciousness of social dynamics developed. Why are most blacks poor and most whites rich? Why are there white elections in which a black person cannot participate, yet when the elections are over and those elected make decisions, they affect me as well? Why should I be hunted by the police for a *dompas* while I was a student?

All black children had to have the *dompas* at the age of sixteen so their movements could be regulated. For the police it was guesswork whether a child walking along a street in Soweto was sixteen or younger, so what they did was arrest anyone they thought tall enough to be sixteen. It rested on the child to prove that he was younger. He was kept in custody until his parents or relatives arrived with a birth certificate.

When we were on an evangelistic mission in the Witbank area, we worked with people who were threatened daily by raids for permits allowing them to be in that area. Only workers registered with some white "boss" were permitted to be there. The families, of course, were also not allowed to be there unless they were all employed. Why? Why did this apply only to blacks and not to whites?

I could continue with all sorts of questions that arose in this regard, but the most serious were questions raised during our reading of the history of mission in South Africa and the history of the white settler community since 1652. For those who do not know

South African history as it is presented in schools and black universities, it is a history of the land from the point of view of this settler community and its descendants. We appear on the scene only when they make contact with us, especially when a conflict of interests occurs.

During school we heard very little, if anything at all, about the history of the black struggle against European settlers who undertook an extensive program of dispossession of blacks—of their land, livestock and so forth. Their program was taken to its logical conclusion by the Nationalist Party. We heard almost nothing about the African National Congress (ANC), the 1955 Congress of the People, the Freedom Charter, the Pan-Africanist Congress. We did not hear much about the gallant struggles waged by Albert Luthuli and that he became a Nobel Peace Prize Winner. We heard nothing of the gallant struggles of the Mandelas, of the warning that if the apartheid regime persisted with its declaration of South Africa as a Republic without involving the majority of its people, it would be a disaster for the future of this country.

But in the history of European settlers in South Africa we were told that when the trekkers moved into the interior, they prayed God to help them defeat our people. At the battle of Blood River, in fact, they made a covenant with God that if God would help them defeat the Zulus and take their land, they would build a church for God. Indeed, after this battle, where many of our people were killed because of the inferior arms they had, compared with the trekkers' gunpowder, they built a church and later declared that day a day of the covenant. That holiday is still in our calendar today as a witness against the God of life.

I could cite many other examples but, during my secondary-school days, the question of whites who claimed to have been helped to subdue us by God was pertinent to our conception of faith. Are whites richer and do they dominate us because God loves them better than us? Did they defeat our forefathers and mothers because God was on their side? Is God with us or with the oppressors? If God is on the side of the oppressor, can the oppressed worship that God and pray to that God to save them from the merciless oppressor? Is this God not the white man's and white woman's God, the God of the oppressors, the God of exploitation, the God of the dominant classes in society, the God of war and of the violence of the powerful in society? This must be a racist God.

The conception of my schoolmates was that whites—Europeans—came and exchanged our land and our freedom for the Bible: that our forefathers and mothers were taught to be humble, submissive and accepting in the name of Christianity so these white racists could subdue them with the least possible resistance. Indeed, there are historical instances I could cite to show that some of the colonialists arranged for missionaries to be brought in advance to clear the way for them to colonize the people.

My schoolmates began to see religion as an opiate of the people, a term known to us from other English literature besides that of Marx. In those days there were no books by or about Marx available to us. That religion was the opiate of the people was a conclusion reached because of the concrete historical situation people confronted, not because of Marx. They wanted to make sense of this reality. To them, therefore, to be a Christian was to help the minority white racist regime continue to oppress the people. It was an act of collaboration and cooperation with the enemy. Mission work was inevitably seen as part and parcel of the strategy to make blacks as submissive as possible, to brainwash them to accept their oppression.

It was during this period that my faith was badly shaken, shaken to the roots. Being a member of the Student Christian Movement (SCM), which did not seem to bother about the sociopolitical, historical and material realities of our situation, appeared to be an act of selling out. Thus most of us were ashamed of associating with the SCM, although I was still very active in the church at home. To avoid this schizophrenic state of mind, some of us decided to risk participating in the SCM to try to make sense of our faith. In 1969 I was elected as chairperson of the SCM during my last year of study for the Junior Certificate.

An emphasis on the preaching of the Gospel of individual salvation was also undergoing an upswing at the time, both in our communities and in the SCM. The emphasis was on the need to be "born again," to be changed into a "new creature," a new person, a child of God. So there was a need to repent, to go through a process of conscious personal commitment, to confess one's sins and be forgiven, washed, cleansed with the blood of Jesus. Romans

3:23, 1 John 1:8–10 and 2 Corinthians 5:17 became key texts in our mission. I remember us inviting SCM members at Orlando West High School to come and share a program with us. Caesar Molebatsi was the preacher that day and made all this new input to our faith make more sense.

But, however helpful this emphasis was in helping us set our spiritual lives right with God, it did not address the contradictions referred to above. Although, through this highly evangelical faith, we could see that those white oppressors who claimed to be Christian could not be living according to this view of faith and Christianity, it did not help us to address and explain the South African situation. We managed to say that what whites were doing to blacks was not Christian, but we still could not absolve the faith from the blame.

It was only during my high-school education at Orlando High School that an attempt was made to address these contradictions. The clash between Christian students and other students on this issue reached a violent level in 1971, my last year at Orlando High School. After the clash, a mass meeting of the warring factions was called, involving some of the teachers as well, to try to resolve this issue. I was asked to address this meeting.

This forced me to find some answers for these problems. I grappled with the reality that the Bible was indeed used to dispossess us of our land, that it was used to brainwash the people, but I advanced the argument that this was in fact a misuse of the Bible and a misrepresentation of the Christian faith. We had to choose between rejecting it because it was misused or take responsibility for reappropriating the Bible, putting it in its rightful place, and reinterpreting it. The slogan was therefore: ''Reread the Bible and reinterpret it in the light of the truth, and turn it against the oppressors.''

This was a new dimension in my life as a young Christian in apartheid South Africa. I began to be jealous about the misuse of the Word of God to justify the *status quo*. I began to be jealous of the use of Christianity to legitimize existing evil systems. I became angry that this trend, this white form of Christianity, was nullifying Jesus' work on the Cross, that it raised the question of the credibility of the mission of Jesus Christ in this world. To me the most serious sin was this sin of subverting the very mission of God in this world by creating a situation where millions of blacks would fail to believe.

At the University of the North in Pietersburg, the SCM was banned from the campus by resolution of the student body because the students believed that it was a religion of the oppressor, of the white man, and therefore worse than irrelevant for them. The Christian group we found there worshiped and prayed on a nearby hill or used a lecture hall illegally. They saw this act of the student body as an act of persecution against Christians and felt great that they were suffering for the sake of the Lord. The more they were pressured by the student body, the more they became convinced they were persecuted, and the more pious they became. When I arrived there in 1972, I felt that I could not identify with this attitude. The Christian students were demonstrating the fruit of what the oppressors wanted to achieve: to make them so spiritual that they would not worry about "earthly things," and so make it easier for them to continue oppressing and exploiting us.

After demonstrating our rejection of the SCM position for almost a year, some of us were invited to participate in the election of a new committee for the period 1972–1973. Cyril Ramaphosa, now general secretary of the National Union of Mineworkers (NUM), was elected SCM chairperson. He was a gifted administrator. He restructured the whole organization and introduced a new constitution that rejected racism and the unjust system of apartheid in the section on "doctrinal basis." It was on this basis of this new constitution and structure that I was elected as a chairperson of the Evangelistic Fellowship, the SCM's mission department. Lybon Mabasa served as my vice-chairperson.

Through the programs of this Evangelistic Fellowship we brought the Christian faith back to the center stage of the life of the student body. We organized public meetings and seminars where we invited people such as the Rev. Maurice Ngakane, who was then the national traveling secretary of the SCM. This was the heyday of the black consciousness movement, and we dealt with themes such as "Christianity and black consciousness." Another person we invited was Rev. Farisani, who is now a dean of the Lutheran church in the Vendaland Bantustan.

Although one would not agree with the findings of the Snyman

Commission about the causes of unrest on campus in 1974, they pick on 1973 as a critical year in their search for its origins. Judge Snyman describes me in the report as a member of the South African Student Organization (SASO) who infiltrated the SCM and used it to agitate students on campus. Of course this was untrue. The fact of the matter is that I had become a member of the SCM while still at secondary school before SASO had even been formed. I only joined SASO in 1972 after registering as a student at the university. Shortly thereafter, SASO was banned on campus by the university administration and stayed banned until the latter part of 1974, just before the FRELIMO rally. Maybe when I gave evidence on behalf of the student body and then as outgoing chairperson of the SCM for the period 1973–1974, the judge simply could not understand the way I was, unless I was a SASO member who had infiltrated the SCM. Anyway, I am proud that I was a member of SASO, and through the SASO experience and this confrontation I was able to develop a better understanding of my faith and present the Christian faith in a critical perspective. But what I want to show is that the judge focused on the Evangelistic Mission because it made an impact in its own right at this time.

Besides the mission to the student body, we also had evangelistic programs in schools, teacher-training institutions, technical colleges, hospitals and to local residents (mostly in rural settings). We covered a radius of almost 100 kilometers around the university. During 1974 we carried our mission to other universities. The most significant was our mission to the University of Zululand. We took along with us Caesar Molebatsi, who is now executive director of Youth Alive Ministries. The debates there centered on the relevance of the Christian faith in the South African situation.

The intervarsity conference of the SCM during the 1974 vacations in Lesotho was a significant conference in terms of broadening this Christian consciousness at a university level. I was asked to present a paper on "Christianity and Black Consciousness." Within two months the Evangelistic Fellowship was invited by the SCM of Lesotho to handle their conference, which again centered on the question of the relevance of the Christian faith for the oppressed black masses of South Africa.

I have related this whole story because for me it constituted part of my struggle to become a Christian in an apartheid society. I tell it simply to show my own struggle and the development of my faith, both of which forced me to reinterpret the whole Christian faith and identified for me the liberating elements in its tradition and in the scriptures.

My Calling and Training
as a Pastor

During my secondary and high school education, I was already involved in one form of ministry or another, both in the church and at school within the SCM. I served as secretary to the church board (parish council) from about 1968 until early 1972, when I left for university. At the end of my high school education, Pastor Mhlongo, one of our senior pastors in the West Rand district of our church, approached me and asked whether I was aware that the Lord was "using me effectively in the church," and that this could be an "indication of God's calling for me." He asked me to consider going for training as a pastor.

My response was that I myself had been grappling with this issue, but then I could not understand why, if God had called me into the ministry—in the traditional sense—I was performing so well in the sciences at school, particularly in mathematics. I could not reconcile the two aspects of my life. I felt that there must be a reason for my good performance in science, and so I decided to go to the university for a BS degree. During my university education I began to explore the subject of science and the Bible, which is usually a burning issue for students at this level. I addressed a number of meetings and conferences on this subject during this time. It seemed to me that I could continue in science as part of my ministry over and above my direct involvement with the church. To me, being a medical doctor, scientist, lawyer, or nurse all were ministries in their own right. All the sciences and professions, in fact, are ideally meant to be at the service of humanity, to transform this world and make it more habitable. In theological terms, this "habitable world" would be the ideal world that God made, where God's justice reigns. Given that something went wrong in

17

the world, we can now only talk about this in eschatological terms, in terms of the coming kingdom of God.

The problem with these sciences and professions, of course, starts when men and women, overwhelmed by self-interest and evil intentions, misuse them, thereby negating their very intention. But it dawned on me that the priestly, pastoral profession and the evangelistic mission of the church, which is intended to lead people to the envisaged kingdom, can also serve a negative role. Haven't ministers of religion served oppressive and fascist regimes in this world? Haven't they supported the racist apartheid system in South Africa with an elaborate theological justification? Hasn't the Church done this elsewhere in its history of missions in this world? We cannot answer these questions honestly without saying yes. Much of this has been done in the name of our Lord Jesus Christ.

In hindsight, though, it is clear that two things compelled me to become directly involved in the mission of God in this world: the need to proclaim the truth of what Jesus died for against all false pretenses, and, precipitated especially by the 1974 events following the FRELIMO rally at the university, the urgency of the situation in South Africa. It is for these reasons that, toward the end of 1974, I began to negotiate with my church to register as a student of their college and train as a pastor.

I now understand just how necessary it was for me to go on with my university studies before training as a pastor. Being at the University of the North at this time was particularly fortunate. The three years I spent there taught me a great deal, particularly about the political situation in the country. Not, of course, because the university offered a course in political science. Even if it did, I doubt it would have been a relevant course for our situation. No, it was the environment.

The period of the early 1970s saw the growth of the black consciousness movement in the universities through the work of SASO. The leadership of SASO consisted then of Steve Biko, who died a martyr's death at the hands of the South African security forces, and Abraham Ongkopotse Tiro, who was killed by a letter bomb in Botswana. It was a time when black students asserted themselves in order to destroy the racist myths that blacks are naturally inferior to whites and that everything black is bad. The black consciousness philosophy talked of the need for both a psychological and physical liberation. We began to reject negative names like ''non-European'' and ''nonwhites.'' We felt we were not the negatives of anybody but black as created by God, in God's image. We began to talk about ''black is beautiful,'' with slogans like ''black power,'' asserting ourselves against the odds, against the dominant ideology of apartheid and racism. Expressions like ''Black man, you are on your own!'' motivated us in this struggle against white paternalism and liberalism.

Having gone through this experience as a member of SASO and lived out the tension of trying to combine SASO and SCM membership, I would never be the same again. I left the university after three years better prepared to undertake the ministry I am involved in today. What was more important was the experience rather than the certificate—that I did not get, anyway. I feel now that it was as if God had sent me into the wilderness like Moses to enable me to handle the wilderness experience that was to come later.

Nevertheless, I did finally decide to train as a pastor of my church. But why then? And why choose to practice after Turfloop in the Apostolic Faith Mission, which seemed quite conservative, and which was dominated by Afrikaners who were part and parcel of the system of apartheid or its beneficiaries? How did I expect to survive? These are questions many people ask me.

Well, it is simple. This is the church within which I was brought up. But there is something more than that. It was the depth of its spirituality that appealed to me. However narrow and shallow this could be, it is this depth of spirituality: a complete trust in the Lord, faith in the death and resurrection of the Lord, faith in the power of the Cross, that has carried me through all my times of trial. It is this evangelical faith that has made me take seriously the eschatological dimension of the Gospel.

How did I expect to survive? Well, I went in by faith, believing that God would take care of the situation. Whatever happened to me did not matter. What mattered was that God had called me to minister to the people of South Africa through the Apostolic Faith Mission as a vehicle for his mission. And I did.

Although there were graduate schools for whites, there were none for blacks. The only single postgraduate college available to black Africans was at Potgietersrust in the northern Transvaal. When I visited the college in 1974, I found a college with only one lecturer teaching students ranging from those with very little academic qualifications to a few college graduates. For this reason, and because of some personal pressure from home, I requested a correspondence course.

For the first few months of 1975, I taught mathematics and physical science at Naledi High School as a private teacher. During this time I met some of the student leaders of Soweto 1976: Khotso Seatlholo, who is now serving a ten-year sentence and who followed Tsietsi Mashinini in the leadership of the Soweto students. He was in my class along with Hlatshwayo, who is also serving a long term of imprisonment on Robben Island and played an important leadership role in Kagiso, Krugersdorp. Although I did not personally teach him, there was also Enos Ngutshana, who played an important role in the student revolt of 1976. By being involved during these few months in both the SCM and the debating society, I learned of the qualities of such students; they showed a high level of political consciousness, quoting widely from Kwame Nkrumah, Julius Nyerere and others.

During the year before May 1976, I worked with Christ for All Nations, the evangelistic organization of Pastor Reinhard Bonnke. A German missionary, he had started Christ for All Nations when working with our church in Lesotho and, in 1975, decided to extend his ministry to the whole southern Africa region. He negotiated with me through Pastor Gschwend, the mission director of our church, as early as 1974, to join him in this mission after he became based in South Africa.

Maybe I should help you understand the structure of our church, which has not changed much since then. We have a white church with its own executive committee and its president who is elected solely by them. This white church appoints a missions director who takes responsibility for what are called ''daughter'' churches or the ''mission churches.'' These are the so-called African, Colored and Indian churches. In fact the missions director chaired the national executive councils of these daughter churches. Technically, according to the constitutions of these churches, they were merely an extension of the mother church. The real church was the mother church, and we were just a mission field of this church.

The first time I encountered a serious problem with this structure was when I said to my dad, who was then an elder in charge of our congregation: "Dad, I would like to join Pastor Gschwend* as a missionary to preach the Gospel to the world." Then I discovered that structurally this was not possible. According to this classical, traditional concept of mission, Europeans or Americans or "whites" in South Africa were the only people who could be called missionaries or work as missionaries. Those who were the objects of missions, i.e. blacks in South Africa, could only be assistants in this mission to their people. So when Pastor Gschwend approached me to work with Pastor Bonnke, it seemed to be a bridge to get beyond the obstruction of apartheid structures in the church.

My meeting with Pastor Gschwend was too dramatic to forget. He made an appointment with me to meet him in Pietersburg, where he was going to attend a meeting, and gave me an address of a white pastor of the white church in Pietersburg. When I arrived at the house, I knocked at the front door. A black woman appeared at the door, asked for my name and what I wanted, and then said to me, "No, there is no such person in this house." I insisted that Pastor Gschwend said that I would meet him at the house. She then said, "Let me call the 'missies'," closing the door behind her. The "missies," who happened to be the local pastor's wife, opened the door after some minutes and said to me, "What do you want?" I explained my story again. She then told me that Pastor Gschwend and the local pastor were still at a meeting at the church. I asked whether I could wait for them, and she said that she did not know as she did not know how long they were going to be at the church. After saying that I was quite happy to wait, as this was the place he had agreed with me, she told me that I could wait outside and not in the house. Feeling hurt, I drifted in the direction of the church, where I found them closing the meeting, and went back to the house.

This event reminded me of a visit with my father to our district missionary chairperson. My father was in charge of a congregation in Soweto, but when we arrived at the house in Krugersdorp we were told to go to the back door. At the back door we were shown a garage where we were to meet the pastor. *Not in his house. Not for blacks.* I could not understand then why Christians behaved like this, but now I understand.

I spent a very painful and agonizing year with Pastor Bonnke, a

*The missions director.

gifted man who was obviously ordained by God. But he launched his ministry within an apartheid context which was bound to land him in serious contradictions. Although he was allowed to move from Lesotho to South Africa, and although he was allowed to buy a house in Boksburg, he could not bring along Pastor Kodisang simply because of the color of his skin. I remember that Pastor Kodisang had to leave his family in Lesotho and come to South Africa on a one-month permit which had to be renewed monthly, to enable him to continue as Pastor Bonnke's main partner. Pastor Bonnke did not like this whole experience but, in his own words, he could not do anything as a foreigner, lest he be deported.

The second devastating experience for me with Pastor Bonnke occurred right at the beginning, when we found an office in the old Braamfontein Church of the Apostolic Faith Mission, on the corner of Harrison and Juta streets. The white youth department of the church was already occupying some of the offices when we arrived. For the first few months, Pastor Bonnke traveled extensively to set up the mission and find the necessary funds for it. So I occupied the office alone most of the time. The staff of the white youth department shared tea with me during teatime, but I was given tea in a tin mug while they used ordinary cups. Yet when Pastor Bonnke joined me in the office, he got his tea in one of their cups, while I was made to use the tin mug. I remember Pastor Bonnke looking at his cup, looking at my mug and then saying, "Let's go shopping." He bought cups for us to avoid the problem of those racist white Christians.

But this was not the end of it. The next thing that happened was that I was told not to use the toilet just next to the door of my office, but the one on the top floor. I could not understand the logic of this, so I continued to use it. Then a special delegation was sent to tell me that these fellow "Christians" were upset that I had continued using the toilet when they had asked me not to use it. This was apparently because my skin was black. I told the messenger that I did not see sense in what they were saying. I did not expect Christians to think like that. I felt that if they gave us offices there, it was my right to use the toilet. The next thing to happen was that a lock was put on the toilet, and all those with white skins were given duplicates of the key. When Pastor Bonnke came back, he could not understand why the toilet was locked. But later he discovered that all this was because I had to be barred from sharing a toilet with them, our fellow "Christians."

The climax came when the war broke out in Angola between the MPLA and Savimbi's UNITA and the FLNA of Holden Roberto. This strange Christian community at Braamfontein, who could not drink tea with me from the same cup and could not share a toilet with me, invited me to share with them in a prayer meeting. They were going to pray for Angola and the South African forces that were now involved in this war. They wanted to pray that Angola should not be taken by "Communists," that is the MPLA, and they saw it as their responsibility to pray for those forces fighting against the MPLA. I, of course, refused to join them. I demanded that before we prayed about Angola, hundreds of miles away, we first needed to pray about the toilet that was next to my office door. Anyway, even if we had to engage ourselves in prayers about Angola, I said, we would have to analyze the situation first, and I doubted we would agree in our perception of the problem. I saw apartheid as the most pertinent issue that was making many Christians act less than Christian, while they saw "Communism" as a major problem.

Today I would express the problem as that of idolatry. This is the greatest threat to our faith and supersedes the problem of atheism. In the tradition of the Bible, God is concerned more with the harlot Israel than with the other nations. And he is concerned more with Israel's idolatry than with the religions practiced by the other nations.

There were two major issues that caused me to part with Pastor Bonnke after working together for only one year. The first was the type of letters I received from white Christians directed to Christ for All Nations. The call was, "Please come and have an evangelistic campaign in our area because there are many 'terrorists' and 'Communists' here." The most glaring of these letters came from the Vaal Triangle and referred to Sebokeng as "terrorist-infested." "Terrorists" and "Communists" in this context mean those blacks who were resisting the apartheid system.

From these letters I realized that many whites in South Africa had a different perception and concept of mission from that of advancing the kingdom of God. Their concept of mission was making blacks accept the *status quo,* be obedient to their masters, and not steal from them. This, of course, was not what I was called for.

I also realized that my presence around Pastor Bonnke—with my track record with the apartheid security forces, coupled with my student ministry which was very critical of the system—could jeopardize his ministry. Intelligence agents could focus on him and maybe bring about his deportation. I felt that I did not want to be responsible for that. If it had to happen, it had to come from his own witness against sin in this evil society.

For these reasons and because my ministry was almost reduced to ordinary office and clerical work, I resigned from Christ for All Nations and joined the West Rand district of my church as an evangelist. My assignment was to establish new congregations and undertake training in leadership before a pastor was placed there. By now I had almost completed half my pastoral training, and I was soon placed in a congregation to begin practicing as a pastor under the supervision of one of the senior pastors of our district. This provided a very unique form of training, giving me a lot of practical experience in the ministry. I completed the course in 1979 and was put on probation until early 1980, when I was ordained.

Balancing the Pendulum

Right from the start, when I committed myself to take up pastoral work with my church, I was well aware that there was a dimension of this ministry which was lacking in the whole concept of mission in my church. I was aware of the overemphasis on the spiritual-vertical relationship with God—over and above the social-horizontal dimension. Of course, I must thank the Lord for putting me through this form of spirituality, despite its inadequacies, because I am who I am today because of this grounding. I am pleased that I was confronted with the need to repent, to surrender my everything, my life, to the Lord: to be "born again," be a "new creature," "baptized and filled with the Spirit," and to strive to live a "perfect" spiritual life in preparation for the imminent kingdom of God. So when it comes to the evangelical and Pentecostal faith, I can say like Paul that if any person thinks she or he has reason for confidence in the Spirit, I have more: born and brought up by a devout Pentecostal family, a Pentecostal of Pentecostals; as to evangelism, an evangelist at heart and, as to God's power, a believer in the works and deeds of power in the name of the Lord.

But when the reality of the South African situation confronted me, I realized that I needed a deeper form of spirituality beyond my classic evangelical and Pentecostal training. The problem is, of course, that churches tend to emphasize one dimension of our faith at the expense of another. Thus, to cross over from one church to another to deal with this inadequacy might just mean turning the pendulum through 180 degrees. There was the risk of moving from an overemphasis on the spiritual to an overemphasis on the social, one at the expense of the other. For this reason I chose to stick with my church and introduce the mission dimension. This also meant developing a new theological basis for this venture and experience. The name of the game was *balancing the pendulum*.

This idea was expressed better in the preamble to the constitution of the Interdenominational Youth Christian Club (IYCC) based in Kagiso, Krugersdorp. The formation of the club was part of my struggle to try to develop this new vision of a balanced ministry. The preamble reads as follows:

> Whereas we cannot simply dismiss the fact that, although the church in South Africa has been misused by the still prevalent satanic agencies that lead to the overwhelming rejection of the Christian faith by the disillusioned black masses, the church has contributed partly to enable us to reach the truths as laid down by the Holy Scriptures, we note with regret that there are two streams of the church that have failed to see the gospel as meant for the "total man"—the Spiritual and Social man—as preached by Christ.
>
> Besides the aims and objects as laid down in the constitution below, we stand and we shall stand to balance the pendulum of the two extremes and tell the truths of the gospel as they are . . . not only preach them but put them into effect as demanded by the Scriptures irrespective of the threatening powers of evil.
>
> We uphold the mission both to reach all the spiritual needs of all men to enter into the Glory of the Lord, and to compassionately extend our hands to any needy persons socially, and strive to establish a "like heaven" earth based on LOVE, JUSTICE and RIGHTEOUSNESS.

The first and main aim of the club read: "To preach the gospel of Jesus Christ, and to urge members to devote themselves to the extension of the kingdom of God within their own environment and throughout the world by brotherly service and evangelistic service."

I would have theological difficulties now with some parts of this preamble, particularly with its sexist language. But it is about nine years ago that it was drawn up, and since then I have travelled a long, long road to where I am now. What is important is to note the struggle I was going through.

You will remember that before I started my formal ministry in my church, I passed through a lay ministry as part of a local congregation, leading Sunday school and youth ministries, and I continued this work after joining Christ for All Nations. It would be true to say that in this period I was put on the frontline of all the contradictions inherent in this one-dimensional ministry. In the year before the student uprising of June 16, 1976, I used to hold morning devotions with some of the secondary and high schools in Soweto and received SCM invitations to go to schools and universities around the country. But by far the most dramatic experience for me occurred at Morris Isaacson High School in Central Western Jabavu, Soweto.

After holding morning devotions with the whole school, I was asked to address a special meeting organized by the SCM one afternoon. In it I tried to deal with the relevance of the Christian faith in the South African situation. During the question time, I was confronted by some of the students about the validity of my presentation. They confronted me with the history of Christianity here and elsewhere, its collaboration with oppressive colonial systems, and the usual argument of how the missionaries gave us the Bible and took our land. They argued that the church supported and participated in building up apartheid, or, at the least, condoned apartheid and its evils. Although I tried to answer these questions, one of the students climbed on a chair and called me a ''nonwhite.'' That was the name for collaborators then, blacks with no consciousness of their own but just a reflection—and victim—of the white system. They saw me as brainwashed, with no mind of my own.

I went through the insults boldly, suppressed my emotions, and invited those who had problems to continue the discussion with me after the meeting. The meeting had gone from 2:30 P.M. to 5:00 P.M. From 5:30 P.M. until 8:00 P.M. I got tied up in an endless heated debate in which I argued in defense of my approach of reinterpreting the Gospel and rereading the Bible to discover its liberating themes. I said to them that whites, in fact, had misused the Bible and misrepresented it to serve their own interests. It might be interesting for the reader to know that one of those students happened to be one of the first student leaders in the 1976 student uprisings.

Although we ended on a friendly note and made sure that everyone walked safely home that night, it had become more clear to me that there was a serious problem about the Christian faith in South Africa. The practice of the church in the past was militating against its very own mission. And unless the Gospel was freed from those who had imprisoned it, there was no hope for the church in South Africa.

I remember it was around this time that I preached at an Apostolic Faith mission church in Rockville, Soweto, just after the freedom of Mozambique. The church in Mozambique had collaborated with the oppressive colonial power, going as far as giving its security forces communion in their churches before they went to war against the black people of Mozambique. Because of this collaboration, FRELIMO closed down some of the churches and used them as social centers, nurseries, and so forth. In my sermon I said that unless the church in South Africa changed its stance in relation to the apartheid regime, it would suffer the same fate as the church in Mozambique. And I said that when this happens we should not call it persecution or blame it on the so-called Communists. But we must assume responsibility for it, as a just reward for our deeds and conduct. You can imagine the reaction that I got.

After I had joined the West Rand district of my church in May 1976, I spent a month in Mabieskraal. My work as an evangelist consisted of running revival programs for some congregations, giving training in administration to others, and establishing new congregations. Within a month I had been transferred to Kagiso, Krugersdorp, to do this work while another pastor was being found. But this never happened, because the congregation called me to be their pastor. Nevertheless, I kept up this evangelistic work outside my congregation on a smaller scale than had been initially envisaged.

My first impressions of Kagiso still remain in my mind. They were dramatic and traumatic. I started my work barely a week or so before June 16, 1976. By the week after June 16, every government building, bottle store, bar and shop had disappeared, burned to the ground or destroyed. The township was suddenly full of police and activity. The congregation came to church that day not just to listen to this interesting new pastor again, but as if they were pulling out from a battleground to a place of refuge. They needed to feel secure in this threatening situation.

This was not just a single event. It was a new chapter in my new ministry in the township, a chapter of ministering in an intensified conflict situation. To acquaint myself with the community I had to minister to and understand what made them tick, I visited various people, particularly the legitimate leadership of the community. Six months later most of these people and others disappeared. Their families came to me and asked me to help trace their whereabouts. To meet their needs, I engaged a firm of lawyers who sent letters to the police inquiring about their whereabouts.

Detention and Torture

Whenever the lawyers wrote to the police—and it was often, as many people and children had disappeared—they used my name as the person who had instructed them on behalf of the families. About six months later, on June 6, 1977, the police descended on the manse in the early hours of the morning and took me away after an extensive search. Midmorning of that day, my interrogation started.

From the nature of the questions, it became clear to me that the police were convinced I would not be helping these families without being involved with those who were detained or without knowing what they had been doing. If you minister to them, you must be party to their "crime," so went their logic. Secondly, from the evidence of one state witness in a trial started a year after these people had been detained, it was clear that they had tortured some of the young people to make them give statements incriminating me and so justifying their logic and conviction.

All this caused me to go through a six-week session of physical torture and interrogation. The torture involved being forced to remain in certain contorted positions for many hours until the body gave in. When I could not keep the prescribed position any longer, I was assaulted with fists and various other objects, like a broomstick. At times I was chained against other objects in a crouching position, handcuffs on my feet, and left in that position for a very long time. Once I was hung head down with my hands and feet over a wooden stick and assaulted in that position. I do not remember much of the details of the latter experience, as it looks like I lost consciousness.

Afterwards I was confused, with my whole body completely unstable. Walking was a struggle, and when I arrived at the prison where I was kept, I could not stand steadily as the warders checked me into the prison. I remember the prison warders making a laughingstock of me, saying I had gone through some good "music" and that I was continuing to "dance." The last ordeal of my six weeks of torture had involved being kept standing in one spot for fifty hours continuously without sleep. I was chained against the bars of the heating system, underfed, interrogated and assaulted continuously by teams of interrogators who changed shifts every eight hours, twenty-four hours around the clock.

During this ordeal, I tried to make sense of the Gospel and the sermons I preached about loving your enemies. I began to ask questions as to what all this meant in this situation. I began to ask questions about God's power and concern. I began to wonder why God could allow these people to do this to me. Does God really care? I began to ask whether the deeds of power of the times of Jesus and the early church were not applicable in our situation. And why?

One thing that kept me strong and made me survive was the experience of the Lord Jesus Christ: for the salvation of the world, it did not seem Jesus could have let the cup pass. He had to drink of the cup for our sakes. He was forsaken for our sakes.

The experience of the apostles also kept me strong. It does not seem the Gospel we have today could have been passed to us without them going through the persecution they suffered even unto death. Peter's words were encouraging: "If you have to suffer for righteousness' sake, you will be blessed. Have no fear of them, nor be troubled, but in your hearts reverence Christ as Lord . . . be prepared to make a defense to anyone who calls you to account for the hope that is in you, yet do it with gentleness and reverence . . . keep your conscience clear so that when you are abused those who revile your good behavior in Christ may be put to shame" (1 Peter 3:14–16).

Peter goes on to say that "it is better to suffer for doing right, if that should be God's will, than for doing wrong" (v.17). "For Christ also died," he says, "for sin once and for all . . . that he might bring us to God" (v.18). In 1 Peter 4:13 he comes up with the most difficult but most empowering word: "Rejoice in so far as you share in Christ's suffering so that you may also rejoice and be glad when his glory is revealed." Paul takes Peter's exhortation a bit further by saying, "Now I rejoice in my suffering for your sake, and in my flesh I complete what is lacking in Christ's afflictions for the sake of his body, that is, the church'' (Colossians 1:24). Complete what is lacking in Christ's afflictions? What does Paul mean? Does he mean that Christ has not completed his work on the Cross? Does he mean that there is something lacking in Christ's work on the Cross?

On the surface this word *lacking* seemed to suggest some form of arrogance in Paul which bordered on heresy. Exegetes are not agreed as to how Paul helps to complete the sufferings of Christ. But as I went through the pain I began to understand that, in fact, Christians have an enormous responsibility to the world, far more than they are aware of: Christ suffered and called us to be prepared to suffer to complete the work he had started by laying down his life for the world. This seemingly heretical statement of Paul expresses his awareness of the fact that Jesus died only ''once for all,'' as Peter says (1 Peter 3:18), but this mission he has started can only be advanced further to its completion if we are prepared, during our time, to be afflicted for his part. When the Gospel is at stake in this evil world, it is our responsibility to stand up and be counted for the sake of the afflicted body of Christ.

The more I tried to interpret what Paul was trying to say, the more jealous I became about the body of Christ. I felt that Christ could not suffer in vain. I felt it was a matter of life and death for me to suffer for the sake of others, the weak in our society, the brutalized, for the sake of Christ's body—that is, his Church. I felt more empowered to say to my torturers during my fifty-hour ordeal, men who had told me I was going to die ''slowly but sure,'' that ''FOR ME TO LIVE IS CHRIST, AND TO DIE IS GAIN'' (Philippians 1:21). ''For Christ will be honored in my body whether by life or by death'' (v. 20).

I said to them: ''If I die now, I will be with the Lord. This is gain for me and even for the kingdom.'' But if they let me live, I would still have to live for Christ, and it would mean continuing to challenge the evil apartheid system in South Africa. It was like using Mandela's words: ''If you release me I will start where you stopped me as long as this evil system still exists.''

My torturers had asked me in the course of this ordeal to make a choice between dying slowly in a painful way and cooperating by collaborating with them against those I am called to minister to. I told them that collaboration and cooperation with the evil racist system in South Africa was out for me. This to me was equal to a call for me to abandon the very fundamentals of my faith and calling. I told them that instead they had to decide whether to let me die or live, being conscious of the consequences of both options. Later, on rereading Paul, I realized that in verse 29 he was uncertain as to which option he would choose. But I did not have to make the choice; it lay in their hands. Through pain they made me feel at one stage that if I were to die, then the faster the better.

At one stage they suggested that I should commit suicide to speed up my death. My response was that Frank Chikane did not have the right to take his own life, and, anyway, I was not going to let them off the hook by terminating my own life and make them feel less guilty after what they had done. I felt that if they chose to do it, they must take the responsiblity, and they must face the Lord on the day of judgment.

By the forty-eighth hour, I no longer felt normal enough to be able to continue intelligently answering their questions, and I decided to keep quiet after telling them about my position. I announced that I was not going to answer questions anymore. For two hours they tried every method to force me to talk, but in vain. On the fiftieth hour I was loosened and driven from Krugersdorp to Rustenburg prison, where I was dumped until around January 12, 1978.

When I arrived at the prison with my feet swollen and my whole body aching, I asked to see a doctor before I was locked up in a cell. I was taken to a prison doctor who looked at me, touched my swollen feet and said, ''Just take him to the cell and let him rest. He will be okay.'' No medication was given and no records were made about my condition. I was shocked but I could do nothing. I was completely at their mercy. Although it was difficult that evening for me to sleep because of pain, when I did sleep I almost slept like a dead man.

Throughout my time in Rustenburg prison I was kept in solitary confinement without access to a lawyer or visits by the family. I was not allowed any reading material. The Bible that my younger sister, Thabile, smuggled into Krugersdorp prison was left there when I was transferred to Rustenburg. It took me about three months of arguing with the magistrates who visited me once every three weeks, according to the regulations, before I got a copy of the

Bible. The security police's argument was that they would not give me a Bible because *"dit maak jou 'n terrorist"* ("it makes you a terrorist"). They felt that the Bible did not seem to help me. It is clear that for them, like all oppressive regimes, the Bible helps you only if it makes you submissive to the dictates of the oppressor. When, at last, they did give me a copy of the Bible, they gave me an Afrikaans one, maybe to force me to read their language. But nevertheless it was a blessing to have a Bible, whatever the language.

My release in January 1978 was very dramatic. They brought me to court with six other people, most of whom I was seeing for the first time. In court we were told that we were going to be charged with "public violence." I was surprised, because I was never asked questions about public violence during my entire detention, and I was never involved in such acts. But, nonetheless, we were granted bail of 200 Rand each and warned to appear in court six days later. There was no charge sheet and no indication of exactly what I was charged with.

At two o'clock in the morning of the day we were due to appear, I was redetained. This time I was assaulted right from the bedroom. My chief deacon, Isaac Genu, who stayed in the manse with his family, tried to intervene but was sent back to bed at gunpoint and told to stay there. I was taken away in my pajamas, with my clothes in my hand, and barely was able to pull them on en route to the police station. Besides assaulting me with their fists, they pulled out my hair, and this continued at Kagiso police station, leaving clumps of hair scattered around. Afterwards I was ordered to collect every bit of it and put it in a garbage can. Next I was driven to Bethal, where the trial of some of those detained nearly a year before was in progress. Throughout the journey I was continuously assaulted. By nine o'clock, when we were expected to appear in court in Krugersdorp, we were in Bethal, miles away.

I have never understood why I was redetained that morning, assaulted so badly and driven to Bethal. On our arrival there those who brought us in were ordered to drive us back to Krugersdorp to appear in court. We arrived at 2:00 P.M. The courtroom was packed with members of my congregation, and there I was with my pajamas showing underneath my clothes. To say they were angry to see this unbelievable sight is to understate their real feelings. They were angry. But they became more angry after hearing the magistrate say, *"Daar is nie 'n saak met die man nie"* (''There is no case with this man''). Since that day that congregation was never the same again.

For about two months after this experience I was so upset that I could not sleep in one house for more than two days without feeling vulnerable. Every sound, sight or movement of a car or cars meant that they had come to detain me again, with a high probability of assault and torture. During this time my friends advised me to leave the country because they were convinced that I would not survive another detention, and there was a high possibility of my being killed by the police or other agents of the system. But I felt then that I was called to minister to victims of this very system and leaving the country seemed to me like abandoning the ministry. Although it looked foolish not to follow the advice of my friends, I just felt that God still had a purpose for me in this country and if we all left, no one would be there to minister to the bulk of people who have no option but to face the pain and misery of living under an oppressive, white minority, racist regime.

Social Action and a Struggle with My Church

Before being detained in 1977, we had already conceived of an interdenominational youth group that would broaden our ministry to the whole Kagiso community. Young people from other churches were beginning to attend our Sunday afternoon youth service. While in prison I developed this vision of a community project as a way of balancing the pendulum and extending the limited spiritual ministry of my church into social spheres. On my release, I realized that it would take longer for the church board to share this vision than I anticipated, and I decided to use youth as a vehicle for undertaking this ministry.

The Interdenominational Youth Christian Club (IYCC) formed in April 1978 was committed to balancing "the pendulum of the two extremes" of the church with a department of social welfare and a second department for mission and evangelism. Each committee was directly responsible to the club's executive committee. When I proposed the community project to the latter in October 1978, they took it up with great enthusiasm. Toward the end of the year the South African Council of Churches (SACC) was approached to help finance a survey of the community of Kagiso to determine their most pressing needs.

The survey was undertaken during the first quarter of 1979. About two thousand houses, one-third of all the houses in Kagiso, were covered by members of the youth club, who were given the necessary training by other experienced community workers and social workers. To reinforce the young people in Kagiso, members of Youth Alive and Teen Outreach Christian Youth Club from Soweto were brought in to participate in the survey.

Among many issues reflected in the results, the following emerged as the most pressing needs and problems of the community: unemployment, the housing crisis, educational problems, problems of child care and help for the aged, and the complexities of the apartheid laws for people who had little grasp of how to handle them. Out of this survey, meetings of people affected by and interested in specific problem areas were called to enable them to discuss and develop strategies for dealing with them. Out of these meetings came committees to undertake the following projects: an information office that later became an advice office; sewing and knitting projects; a project for the blind; upgrading classes for matriculants and an adult-education program; a child-minders' project; and a project on care for the aged.

The congregation offered one corner of its small church as an office for the project, while the whole church was occupied by project participants whenever there was no church service. Later a structure was built for this purpose in the yard of the church.

The development of this project forced me to grapple with the theological issues of integrating the spiritual and social dimensions of the ministry of the church. Out of this experience of practice (praxis) came of necessity a comprehensive theology of mission. It also pushed me to look for literature that would help my thinking. The project in addition helped both the youth and the congregation to understand their mission as Christians more fully. From it came leadership skills for many of the school-age youth; they and some of the adult participants were later to play important leadership roles in the schools and community, especially during times of crisis. The advice office began to play an important role, linking the community with other resource organizations like the SACC, particularly its Dependants' Conference, the Black Sash, the Legal Resources Center, and so on.

In short, that small "white church"—called so because it was painted white outside—on the outskirts of Kagiso became the community's lifeline, especially in times of crisis. Even "lost" people were sent to the church. Of course, we paid heavily for this ministry because whenever there was a security police blitz or raid in Kagiso, we would be the first targets. In fact the police treated our church as enemy number one in Kagiso. At one stage I also began to feel that I was regarded as enemy number one in the whole Kagiso community. What worried the police most was the influx of people in and out of that church. During questioning at different times, I was asked, "Why do all the young people come to your church rather than others? They are not members of your church," they said. To the police this showed that we were involved in something subversive. To me, of course, this was an indication of the success of our ministry.

The community project was part of a variety of complex factors that were getting me into trouble with my church. Among the most pronounced factors were those stemming from my perception of the mission of the church in apartheid South Africa, my ministry to the community in Kagiso, Krugersdorp, the project, and the related detentions. While a pastor in Kagiso, I was detained four times. The first was for seven days between January and February 1977, when I was badly assaulted for the first two days to a point where I could not walk properly. I have already written about my torture during my second period of detention from June 1977 until January 1978. A few days after my release, I was rearrested and brutally assaulted again.

The third detention was in November 1980 for just a few days when P. W. Botha went to Krugersdorp to receive the "freedom" of the city. This honor was extended to Botha by the Krugersdorp City Council, and they invited the black township dwellers of Krugersdorp through the local dummy Urban Black Council. People in the black township felt that they could not participate in an event which gave P. W. Botha the freedom of the city when they were not free themselves. They were deprived even of their citizenship in the land of their birth. They could not choose where they wanted to stay or work. They could not own land where they stayed. They could not decide on the nature of the local council that would meet their needs, nor could they participate in the election of the government that was governing the country. So the black communities decided to boycott the occasion.

The regime panicked and detained all those blacks who in their opinion were playing a leadership role in the community. We were detained one day before Botha's arrival and released one day after the celebrations. The only way we had a taste of Botha's celebration of the freedom of Krugersdorp was through the sound of sirens that penetrated the walls of the prison depriving us of our freedom.

The fourth detention was just after my one-year suspension by the Church that I describe below. It was in November 1981; it lasted until July 1982, and covered almost all the period of my suspension. Again I was released without being charged.

During my 1977–1978 detention when I was so badly tortured, the district council within whose jurisdiction I was a pastor decided to remove me from my congregation while I was in prison. It now seems that this decision was made under pressure from the white district of the church that was subsidizing the black church. They felt they could not go on subsidizing a district which had a pastor who was detained under the Terrorism Act.

To them, once you were detained under this act you were regarded as a terrorist. This was precisely the strategy of the apartheid system: to detain legitimate leaders of the community for representing or articulating the legitimate grievances of their communities and thereby criminalize them. Once criminalized, they used brutal methods against them. The criminalization process is a preparation for the justification of brutal and inhuman acts against blacks to stop them from resisting their oppression and exploitation.

What is interesting is that this crude form of propaganda works with whites; they benefit from it and from the system it is meant to defend at all costs. But for blacks who know the people who are brutalized and know the noble ideals of justice and peace which are so opposed to the system, this propaganda has the opposite effect. It makes blacks rally around them and support them at all costs. The reaction of the congregation in Kagiso to the suggestion that I be removed *in absentia* reflected this degree of polarization created by the apartheid system. The congregation insisted that the district committee wait until I was released, or until my case was decided in court, before such an action was contemplated. They did not believe that I had committed any criminal act. Knowing me, they could not believe it until it was proved otherwise.

Immediately after my release in January 1978, after the magistrate had thrown my case out, the district committee convened a meeting to carry out their decision, irrespective of the court's finding. The congregation refused to agree to the proposed action of the district committee. The committee responded by withdrawing the subsidy—or travel allowance, as they called it—from the congregation. Then later, in 1979, when I was formally registered as a probationary pastor after completing my course, I was obliged to sign forms guaranteeing that I would not be involved in politics. Every probationary pastor had to sign the same form, so this did not worry me too much, whatever they meant by "politics."

Around January–February 1980, I was summoned by the West Rand district committee to hear a list of accusations. First I was accused of running projects within the church which some did not see as a proper part of our ministry. They felt that I was called to preach the Gospel rather than engage in community projects. Some said that they had information that the church was no longer used for spiritual activities. I imagine this was a deliberate exaggeration to press the point home that I should concentrate my life on what they called the spiritual ministry. Because if it were not a matter of exaggeration, then it would have been a serious matter. We managed to clear up this issue with them accepting my understanding of the ministry, and how to me the social is not a secondary ministry but the very essence of my work as a pastor. My explanation was accepted with reluctance.

I was then accused of being involved in politics. This was because I spoke in meetings at which I was quoted as making "political" statements. Third, I was accused of using my church for political meetings. There were difficulties in dealing with the second count, because when you preach in a student meeting of Christians, you are very likely to be picked up by the press. And if you are invited by groups that are not necessarily Christian, in our situation you cannot say no, otherwise you are closing down the scope of your ministry. In both instances any constraint introduced would militate against the very mission of the church.

The third count was more controversial. While some argued that allowing the community to hold their services at the church was a political act, for me it was offering space for a victimized community that had no facilities for meeting indoors, to meet and talk about their problems, pain and suffering, and how they could handle them. I attended these meetings and services because they affected members of my congregation as much as anyone else. They had housing problems; they had problems of rent, transport, and education for their children. Members of their families were detained without trial, and so on. I felt that if I were not with them, I would be failing in my ministry. At the end of this discussion I was strongly warned not to take part in politics.

In March 1980 I had to undergo an assessment meeting before my ordination. An analysis that I had made of Matthew 22:36–40 had appeared in a newspaper, and, with the newspaper cuttings in front of them, they challenged me on it. The text read as follows: " 'Teacher, which is the greatest commandment of the Law?' Jesus said, 'You shall love the Lord your God with all your heart, and with all your soul, and with all your mind. This is the greatest and first commandment. And the second is like it: You shall love your neighbor as yourself. On these two commandments depend all the law and the prophets'."

To me, this text summed up the problem of the church as I perceived it then. My contention was that the Pentecostal, and most evangelical, churches emphasized the first commandment over and above the second—if they ever worried about it. Other churches concentrated on loving the neighbor without regard for the spiritual life. I argued that if the church was to be church it had to take the last sentence of this text much more seriously: "On these two commandments depend all the law and the prophets."

The bias within my church meant that highly spiritual people who were baptized in the Holy Spirit could see no Christian obligation to struggle against apartheid. Nor did they have any regard for social ethics. Their concern was that my analysis smacked of what is called the "social gospel" within evangelical circles. After a long discussion, they warned me to abstain from political activities and then approved of my ordination.

I made sure that I kept within the specifications of the church's constitution and did not become a member of any political organization, not even the local civic association. But in August 1981 I was confronted by the West Rand district committee, again with a file of press cuttings that was produced as the sole evidence of my involvement in politics. I was involved in politics because I appeared in the newspapers. They provisionally suspended me, pending a decision of the national executive council. The council met in September, followed by the church court in October 1981, which endorsed the decision to suspend me for a year until I repented.

As I have already remarked, I spent most of this period of suspension in detention. On coming back I requested a meeting with the most senior members of the church to review my situation and avoid further problems before the end of my term. Pastor E.

Gschwend, the missions director, organized a meeting with the president of the church, Dr. Möller, and the general secretary of the (white) church. During this meeting I was asked to give guarantees that I would not be detained again, I would not appear in the press again, and I would not be involved in politics. The first two, of course, would be beyond my control; you do not choose to be detained, nor can you evade the press if you are dealing with current matters of our time from a Christian perspective. The third depended on the definition of *politics* of the parties involved. Since our definitions were not the same, it was difficult to envisage a meaningful monitoring of my compliance. We closed the meeting with no solution to the problem.

From October 1982 on, when my suspension had lapsed, I was told that the matter of my reinstatement was on their agenda. Well after a year had gone by and I was still waiting for the results of the committee's deliberations, I received a letter which asked me to return my credentials and my ordination certificate. Realizing that it would be a futile exercise to take the matter further, I surrendered the relevant documentation. By this time I was already involved with the Institute for Contextual Theology, through which I was able to exercise my ministry.

Some people have asked me why I have kept up my membership in the Apostolic Faith Mission. There are two reasons besides the need of every Christian to belong to a fellowship of believers which, after all, I could have had in another church. The first reason is the executive committee's fear that I would cause a split in the church following my suspension. In the last meeting we had together, I promised that I was not going to start another church and that I would never do so. The reason that I advanced was that I believed God had enough problems with the many churches in the world, and I was not prepared to put another problem into God's hands. Secondly the history of the Church had taught me that the churches were made up of human beings with all their human complexities, and this was what influenced their decisions, so I saw no gain in moving from one church to another.

Today, after a period of years, the struggle that began during my time as a pastor of the Apostolic Faith Mission to break the apartheid structures which divide the church into white, colored, Indian and African churches, is maturing. The struggle to face the reality that racist attitudes and tendencies are incompatible with the Gospel of the Lord is confronting everyone in the church.

The crisis reached a head during the 1986 annual workers' council of the church. A unity commission was later constituted with the aim of bringing the apartheid structures in the church to an end. Proposals were presented to the four racial churches' annual workers' councils. The three black churches (colored, Indian and African) accepted in principle the proposed new constitution, while whites rejected it. This created an acute crisis within my church during 1987 which will intensify as time goes by. My prayer is that my beloved church should recognize the opportunity (kairos) that God is offering them, lest God's judgment falls on them.

We need to be alive to the reality that Jesus could not have established the Church without dying on the Cross and being raised again. Thus the Church was born in a struggle of life and death and is plunged into this struggle to work for the kingdom of God. To be Christian is not to relax and enjoy oneself in the midst of sin, corruption, oppression and death. To be Christian means to engage in the struggle for righteousness against unrighteousness, the struggle for justice against injustice, the struggle to save the world. Any view of the Christian life without engaging in struggle cannot be compatible with the work of the Lord on the Cross. Our mission as Christians is to engage in acts of salvation for the world in the name of him who died for it. We are called to proclaim the good news of salvation to the world.

A New Context
for Doing Theology

My five years or so of work with the Institute of Contextual Theology have been highly enriching for me. When I look back over my life, there appears to have been an ordered development from one stage to another which I cannot imagine having happened in any other way. The institute was just the right place for me to systematize and develop my theological understanding of my Christian pastoral experience.

Throughout my life there was never any question of a systematized theory coming before experience; it was always a struggle at a particular time, faced with a particular reality, to determine what role I had to play as a Christian. I struggled with the question of how to undertake the ministry in a range of situations. In the course of this struggle I was forced to look into past and current theological models of life and pastoral work in a variety of situations of conflict throughout the history of the Christian faith. My involvement with the institute made this reading task easier for me. I was able to look at black theology in South Africa and in the USA, and at African theology. I also looked at liberation theology and its development in Latin America. I was exposed to Asian theologies through the Ecumenical Association of Third World Theologians (EATWOT), of which I am a member.

The ministry in a conflict situation project, which involved ministers in the Pretoria-Witwatersrand-Vaal area, helped me a lot to reflect on and share experiences of our situation with other pastors. This group of ministers met once a month for some three years to share and reflect together on their experience of pastoral ministry. Most of these ministers were themselves detained either for short or long periods, and in some instances even tortured by the police,

44

all because of their contact with victims of the apartheid system and their ministry to them. My own experience was typical of what they were going through.

After long periods of reflection and sharing, we reached a consensus that the dominant traditional position, which looked at reality and understood our faith from the point of view of the powerful and dominant forces in society and their ideology (theology) was not compatible with the demands of the Gospel. Surveying the history of the Church since Constantine, we agreed that the Church had taken sides, in the main, with the dominant classes of society, which were principally responsible for the pain, suffering, misery and even death of many, especially the weak, poor and powerless. Since Constantine, the Church had shifted from being a persecuted Church to being the Church of the persecutors. While in the early Christian Church, it had cost the lives of many just to confess that Jesus was the Christ, and for baptism into the Christian faith, after Constantine, not being a Christian put one at risk. The Church was elevated to a position of power, tasted power, and articulated its faith from that position.

It is for this reason that, in the main, the Church failed to see the injustices perpetrated by the powerful and rich against the powerless and poor. One needs only look at the conduct of the Church during the period of colonization and in relation to the struggles of Third World, colonized peoples against colonial powers. The Church tended to take sides with the colonial powers against those who resisted them. We discussed specifically the role of the Church during the czarist regime in Russia and after, its role in the Cuban revolution, in the struggles in Latin America, in the former Portuguese colonies, in South Africa and in Nazi Germany. We also criticized the neutralist position of the Church which, in effect, meant allowing evil, oppression and exploitation to continue unchecked. To us this amounted to collaboration with the forces of evil.

In the light of this analysis our group, which became known as MUCCOR (Ministers United for Christian Co-responsibility), opted for taking sides with the victims of apartheid and for justice. Both MUCCOR and the 1983 ICT conference on this topic were very useful to me in clarifying our theology of taking sides. Our option was in line with the theological model of the Confessing Church in Nazi Germany manifested concretely in the life of Bonhoeffer. It was also in line with many of the Third World theological models emerging from Latin America, Africa and Asia, including that of the black theologians in North America.

As we made this decision we were conscious that we were called to minister to all in the world, both oppressors and oppressed, white and black. The mission of the Church is directed to the whole world, since Jesus died for all. Taking sides with the victims of society in our situation means taking sides with the ideals of the kingdom of God proclaimed by Jesus. This is a kingdom of justice, righteousness and peace, where goodness will always prevail.

Some see a contradiction in this position, but there is no contradiction. What we are doing is calling both oppressor and oppressed, rich and poor, both blacks and whites, to repentance and, in line with the ideals of the kingdom, to take sides with justice against the injustice perpetrated by the oppressors. In South Africa this means taking the side of the blacks against the heresy of white racism. The question of justice here, which is an inherent characteristic of the kingdom of God, goes beyond the question of so-called group interests or the color of particular people. It is justice for all humanity. In trying to explain this position I have often said to blacks that if they took over this country and practiced injustices against whites, or racism in reverse, they would have to detain me as well. I would just have to go back to prison, to the same cell in John Vorster Square, but this time it would be under the control of blacks. We are talking here about the ideals of the kingdom of God.

Looking at the life of Jesus Christ, there can be no doubt about the spirit of his ministry. The famous text of theologians of liberation sums up what Jesus perceived as his mission in the world. It reads: "The spirit of the Lord is upon me, because he has anointed me. He has sent me to preach good news to the poor, to proclaim liberty to captives, and to the blind new sight, to set free those who are oppressed, to proclaim the acceptable year of the Lord" (Luke 4:18, 19).

The problem today is that Jesus is spoken about in terms and values that are totally alien to him. I agree with Albert Nolan that Jesus is wrongly associated with all the things he denounced and rejected. He is associated with kings and lords, with the powerful and important people in society. He is seen as a friend of the upper classes. But did not the historical Jesus refuse to be a king? Did he not choose to identify and live with the poor, the blind, the sick and the hungry, deliberately associating with a rejected class of people in the society of his time? Did he not rebuke the Pharisees, the chief priests and the scribes? Did he not warn the rich that it was easier to pass through the eye of a needle than to enter the kingdom of heaven? Albert Nolan, in his book *Jesus before Christianity* (Orbis:1978), depicts Jesus' attitudes very clearly. Christians cannot just ignore this practice of the Lord Jesus Christ.

I could go on endlessly with a record of how these ideas developed in the context of South Africa and the work of the institute, but I would like to conclude with Jerry Mosala's insights. He argues that the Bible itself is a record of a struggle between the God of justice (Yahweh) and the false gods of injustice. It is a struggle between a God of the oppressor and a God of liberation, between righteousness (goodness) and unrighteousness (sin and evil). His vision of the Bible as a record and a site of class struggle was very helpful to me in trying to understand my role in the conflict-ridden world of apartheid.

The Kairos document grows out of this Christian struggle but takes it a step forward theologically by stating clearly that the two opposing forces are irreconcilable. You cannot reconcile God and the devil, it says. What Christians need to do is remove the evil, fight the devil, and join the forces of good and righteousness in their march into the kingdom of God. It is strongly critical of concepts of reconciliation that suggest injustice can remain while oppressor and oppressed are reconciled cheaply and superficially.

It was inevitable with my Pentecostal and evangelical background that I would try to fit these ideas into my tradition. I looked at the history behind the conflict between evangelicals and ecumenicals. As I tried to balance the pendulum, I could see how much each could enrich the other. Bringing the two streams together needed each tradition to be humble enough to realize that both had some truth that the other lacked and both had weaknesses that needed to be addressed. A humble coming together could help both to develop a higher understanding of the mysteries of the Gospel, as Paul would put it.

The theology program that I went through with the University of South Africa (UNISA) in 1984–1986 helped me consolidate this theological position. But, just as I was forced to abandon my BS degree at the end of 1974, the same fate befell me with the theological degree at UNISA. This is another long story. In short, I found myself outside the country with UNISA adamantly refusing to allow me to take my examination anywhere other than in a South African embassy or consulate. Besides security considerations and my political convictions, I felt that a South African embassy or consulate was not conducive to writing an examination. As we debated this issue, the Geneva consulate, for instance, where I was scheduled to take the examination, was engaged in distributing propaganda literature attacking Dr. Allan Boesak and the people's organizations back home.

For these reasons, despite studying hard, I declined to write, and thus missed getting my degree. Though I am now back home, I have no hope of completing my degree under the present circumstances, and UNISA does not seem to be geared to helping students like us who are victims of the apartheid system. My protest to the senate and council of the university has been totally ignored, and my letters have not even been acknowledged. This is a small part of the price of commitment to the struggles of the people for justice and peace.

Getting Involved with the People's Struggles

Life for blacks in apartheid South Africa is a life of struggle, a struggle for survival and a struggle to be free from the oppressive white minority regime. It is a struggle for survival against a host of apartheid laws that are geared to stifling the lives of blacks. It is a struggle to survive against laws that protect white interests against those of blacks, making whites more privileged than blacks. If there is a black person who has "made it," to use popular language, he or she has really "made it" against the odds.

Just to give an example, my paternal family was forcefully moved twice during my lifetime. Forced removals were part of the grand strategy of land dispossession following the 1913 and 1936 Land Acts. These acts effectively dispossessed blacks of 87 percent of their land, confining them to a meager 13 percent. To use the possessive *our* here is generally a controversial issue in South Africa. According to the history we learned at school, blacks and whites arrived simultaneously in the country. Recent scholarship is diametrically opposed to this thesis. To quote from John Sebidi's article,* archaeological evidence suggests that the arrival of the so-called Bantu south of the Limpopo was much earlier than ethnologists once thought; radio-carbon dating bears testimony to a negroid iron-age settlement in the Transvaal as early as the fifth century A.D.

Enough about our possessive pronoun. My interest here is to explain that blacks were systematically dispossessed of their land and confined to some of the most barren parts of the country to meet

* Sebidi, J. in *The Unquestionable Right to be Free: Essays in Black Theology,* eds. I.J. Mosala and B. Tlhagale (Orbis Books, 1986).

49

the selfish needs of the white settlers. Besides removals, blacks were controlled by influx control laws that made them available only as labor units for the benefit of whites. The 1953 Bantu Education Act makes it clear that black schooling was to train laborers. The Verwoerd speech during the debate on the act in parliament endorses the aims: "We should not give the natives an academic education as some people are prone to do. If we do this . . . who is going to do the manual labour in the country? . . . I am in thorough agreement with the view that we so conduct our schools that the native who attends those schools will know that to a great extent he must be the labourer in the country." *

Today, although we are all equally taxed, we as blacks cannot control the redistribution of this tax. The white parliament makes decisions in our absence, redistributing tax in favor of white interests. Thus the government spends ten times as much per capita on the education of a white child than on a black child, producing the type of education for blacks that Verwoerd intended. Blacks in urban areas are forced to live in ghettos outside the cities so that they cannot—and are not intended to—benefit from the taxes paid by the companies that they work for, which are contributed to the (white) local authorities. I could continue indefinitely talking about the host of laws that limit the life potential of blacks in this country and make the life of blacks a life of struggle.

For generations this struggle has been conducted in an organized form using a variety of strategies. But I was too young in the 1950s and early 1960s to belong to the well-known historic South African liberation movements like the African National Congress and the Pan Africanist Congress, the ANC and PAC. I have only a hazy idea about this period. I have a vague picture in my mind of the frightening vehicles that rumbled along the dusty roads of Soweto during the 1961 strikes. I learned later that they were a form of small tank.

After the events of the early 1960s which were closed by the banning of the two liberation movements, there was a political lull which was followed by the student movement at the end of the

---

*Collins C., and Christie, P., "Bantu Education, Apartheid Ideology, or Labour Reproduction," in *Comparative Education,* vol. 18 (1982), p. 63.

decade. When I became a student of the University of the North in 1972, I joined SASO (the South African Student Organization). My involvement in SASO and in the student politics of the early 1970s shaped much of my political thinking. We needed to assert our humanity in the face of the apartheid system and lose the inferiority complex that the system had instilled. In the black consciousness movement, we found the vehicle to do it. In short, we declared war against the oppressed mind of blacks which was in danger of accepting, or becoming resigned to, its lot and to the status quo.

I have often argued against the emotional outbursts of those who have problems with the contemporary black consciousness movement manifested concretely in the form of the Azanian People's Organization (AZAPO) and who want to suggest that the Black Consciousness Movement (BCM) was, in fact, a reactionary movement trying to divert the people's struggle for liberation. My own experience, and my inquiries with the early proponents of this philosophy—particularly Steve Biko's friends and those who worked with him in his political life—contradict this thesis. The most important of the people that I discussed this point with, and the best known, are Rev. Barney Pityana, who became an Anglican priest in Britain, Rev. Mwalusi Mpumlwana, who is with the Order of Ethiopia Church in South Africa, and Dr. Mji, a past SASO president when the ideological tension within the Black Consciousness Movement began to surface.

My understanding of these events is that they were a natural and necessary political development after the clampdown of the 1960s, and in reaction to the problem of white liberalism. The latter was expressed mainly through the National Union of South African Students (NUSAS), which was attempting to fill the political vacuum of the 1960s. When you analyze the political dynamics in the period from 1968–1969 (when the black consciousness movement started) until 1977, you see an interesting thing happening; white liberalism was sent to the graveyard, as far as the liberation movement was concerned. Honest and concerned whites were forced back to the drawing board. Political scientists would agree that it was during this period that white academics in the English-speaking liberal universities turned more to Marx and the workers' struggle. At the end of this decade we see student leaders within NUSAS and whites outside the student movement emerging into the nonracial democratic movement, using the radical model of social analysis rather than the liberal tradition.

The period of the 1970s was therefore a period of critique of white paternalism and the liberal tradition. This forced both whites and blacks, on their own, to develop a radical model of analysis for our reality so that they met later on equal terms on the basis of a shared understanding. The relationship matured and was now accepted as a matter of critical analysis under the leadership of the African majority. Expressed in class terms, all accepted the leadership of the working class, which is mainly black (or African).

Based on this shared understanding of the 1970s, I believe that the black consciousness movement was a necessary event in the liberation struggle of South Africa. It was a necessary stage for all white liberals to discover their white paternalistic arrogance and move on to join the struggle humbly. It was also a necessary experience for blacks to rediscover their humanity and potential, and to take their destiny into their own hands. This is itself part of a process of liberation, of self-liberation. I am grateful that I have gone through this liberation experience myself. It came as part and parcel of the saving love of God, and has made me take Jesus' work on the Cross more seriously: that Jesus died for me so that I can be saved from death into life, and life more abundant. It has filled my redemption from sin with meaning: I should no longer regard myself as less than the image of God and a complete man, nor should I remain a slave in this society when Jesus has already paid the price of my freedom. It has made me know God's atonement: I should no more be apologetic about my life, but walk tall with absolute confidence, knowing that my shame has been removed.

I therefore see the black consciousness philosophy as a means to an end, but it cannot be an end itself. It is a necessary corrective at a particular stage in our life and history. Faced with a diabolical and dehumanizing system, it counters the process of dehumanization. Otherwise we create a situation where blacks want to turn the pendulum through 180 degrees and exchange white racism for black racism, a white oppressive and exploitative system for a black one.

You will realize that this period was of vital importance for my political and spiritual development. As a pastor of the Apostolic

Faith Mission, I could not be part of any political organization like the Black People's Convention (BPC), which so many students joined when they left the university. The clause in the constitution of the church advised against any such political participation for pastors. Nor could I join AZAPO or the local civic associations in Kagiso and Soweto. The irony was, of course, that although I had stuck strictly to the letter of the law, I was suspended for allegedly participating in politics.

So I had no direct involvement with political organizations between 1974, when I left the university, and 1983. Nevertheless, at various levels, I was directly involved in ministering to those in the midst of these struggles. I believed that I had a special ministry to the victims of apartheid and that, in a theological sense, their political activity could not just be regarded as party politics. The fact of the matter is that we live in a very abnormal situation in which blacks cannot participate in the national political system or in its party politics. Black politics therefore became the politics of protest or resistance against this unjust order. Black politics is the politics of the victims of a white dictatorship and therefore the politics of struggle for justice, rather than the party politics of how to govern justly in the best possible way.

For me the politics of the struggle for justice is part and parcel of the mission of God, and therefore that of the Church and all Christians, while the party politics of how to govern in the best way to build up a more just society is the job of professional politicians. For this reason I identified with the pain and suffering of the black communities to which I was called to minister, even though I did not join their organizations or allow myself to be elected to leadership positions in them. I accompanied them from one crisis to another. It is this identification and solidarity with the victims of the apartheid system that made my church act against me.

It was only in 1983, when I was not directly involved with my church as a pastor, that I became one of the regional vice presidents of the United Democratic Front (UDF). The question that I am often asked is why, as a pastor, I participated in the leadership of the UDF.

There are a number of different reasons. First, when I was released from detention in July 1982, I found that blacks were engaged in a national debate on how they could register their rejection of the proposed new constitution and the so-called Koornhof Bills on black local authorities. To most of us it was clear that the proposed new constitution, which made provision for whites, Coloreds and Indians in a tricameral parliament and excluded the African majority, was a way of further entrenching the apartheid system in South Africa.

The very fact that you had a white parliament voted in by whites only, an Indian parliament voted in by Indians only, and so on, was a clear indication of its racist-ethnic nature. The exclusion of the African majority and the 4:2:1 ratio of whites, Coloreds and Indians was obviously a guarantee of indefinite white domination and power in South Africa. While preserving white economic and political power, for blacks it was meant to co-opt the elite into the system to legitimize the oppressive exploitation of the majority.

The constitutional reforms, however, did not touch the fundamental pillars of apartheid: the Race Classification Act of 1950; the Land Acts of 1913 and 1936; the Group Areas Act; the Citizenship Act and the Separate Amenities Act. With all these still in force, there was no way anyone could claim that apartheid was dead.

The question, then, was what strategies to employ to express rejection of this new apartheid constitution. Two options were debated: the violent and the nonviolent options. Those who argued for the violent option, i.e. for the armed struggle, cited the fifty years of nonviolent struggle of the African National Congress (ANC), and how they were forced to go underground in 1961 after the banning of the ANC and PAC, and only then resorted to sabotage. They felt that it was irresponsible to try the same type of nonviolent strategy, which had resulted in enormous pain, suffering and even the deaths of many people. It seemed as if people had not learned from history.

Of course, when you read Mandela's arguments in court during the treason trial that led to his life imprisonment, you cannot fail to accept that they indeed had no option but to resort to an armed struggle. They had tried all possible methods in vain. They wrote to Malan in 1952, for instance, asking for a roundtable conference to find a solution to the problems confronting the country, but they were ignored. In 1961, when Verwoerd was in power, they asked for a national convention of all the people of South Africa to decide on their future, and again they were ignored. Mandela then says that it was when all other forms of resistance were no longer open to us that they turned to the armed struggle.

Given this unquestionable witness and experience of the Mandelas and Sisulus, it is understandable that any argument to the contrary cannot stand its ground. But those who argued for the second option, the nonviolent option, did not necessarily wish to contradict this tradition of the stalwarts of the South African liberation struggle. Their argument was that there was still room for many South Africans who were not in the armed struggle to participate in nonviolent political activity to oppose the new constitution. I was one of those who argued that political mobilization and organization of the masses against the racist regime was of vital importance to the liberation struggle. I remember using the minister of defense's figures that the military aspect of the total strategy of the state against its enemies only amounted to 20 percent of the total. I argued as well that the political part of our struggle needed to be 80 percent to make any impact, and that a purely militaristic strategy could not bring about our liberation. Using these percentages, I felt therefore that there was a lot of nonviolent activity open to accommodate all those who believed in nonviolence as their contribution to the struggle.

Not that we imagined this would not be a costly venture. I came to believe that there was no way of achieving our freedom without paying a price, whether one opted for the violent or nonviolent method. We had to be prepared to pay the price for this noble goal of a just society. And, of course, we paid heavily for this option.

The debate about the way forward lasted some six months, from July to December of 1982. Because I had argued for a high profile political form of protest to oppose the racist constitution through peaceful means, when the UDF was formed, I was asked to provide leadership for it. Those who participated in the debate put it to me straight: "Come, let us do it together with you," the implication being that you cannot in conscience call for a position and then not participate to demonstrate that it works.

This is the usual problem of the Church. It is usually strong on moralizing, prescribing what methods should be used in striving for change. *But they never try it themselves.* It is like producing tools to be used in the struggle that are never tested. History damns the Church for not having put the nonviolent method to the test itself.

It was left to Martin Luther King, Mahatma Gandhi, and Dom Helder Câmara to engage in concrete nonviolent action to force those in power to redress the grievances of the underdogs in society. The history of nonviolence in the ANC and UDF, following the path of these classic disciples of nonviolent action, must come as an indictment of us in the Church. It exposes our failure and omissions.

A second reason raised to draw me into the UDF was its need for people with credibility among all the political groupings of the oppressed in South Africa, in order to forge the unity required for this mission. Because of the composition of the UDF, which was made up of a variety of groups—churches and church groups, sports associations, community, labor, students', women's, youth and political organizations—I did not find it odd to be involved. To me it was destined to be broad enough to keep me out of classic party politics. But what really made me surrender to this call was the argument that the Church, because of its resources, trains people and then monopolizes them, depriving the peoples' organizations of their leadership. They confronted me with this when I said that I would have problems with my church.

The front brought together a spectrum of peace-loving South Africans who agreed on only one major issue: the apartheid system must go. They needed people in the community with the standing to act as a catalyst and make this broad form of united action become a political reality. It was intended that the front would incorporate the black consciousness movement and what was known as the progressive nonracial democratic movement and church groups. In fact church groups like the Witwatersrand Council of Churches, Diakonia in Durban and Young Christian Students (YCS) did join.

But, although it was difficult to define the broad struggle of blacks as party politics, I still raised some of the traditional problems which might affect my future ministry in my church. I told them about the problem that I had had with my church, about the misconceptions and misunderstandings. My argument was that, even though I was no longer regarded by the Apostolic Faith Mission as a pastor, if I played a leadership role in the UDF, it would reinforce their accusations against me—despite the fact that this would amount to using a future event as part of the evidence for a past event.

My discussions with them frankly raised a lot of frustration and anger, because for them, this was the hour of need. They needed the leadership of the Church and its personnel. To them, my objections meant they were being deprived of leadership when it was in desperately short supply. They accused the Church of picking up their best leadership because of the superior resources at its disposal, thereby acting as a brake on the liberation struggle.

I was already predisposed not to resist these impassioned pleas, because the methodology of doing theology that I had begun to follow—taking an option for involvement, as many Third World theologians were choosing—dictated a further step. Third World theologians today have, in the main, moved from the luxury of just studying theology and theorizing about the people's struggle, from living their faith as an academic or intellectual exercise, to the struggle of doing theology with the people. They start from the premise that theology develops out of the life experience of Christians in the world. In their situation this is a life of struggle for a just society in this world. Is the Bible not a record of stories about the struggles of the children of Israel and people of the time of the early Church concerning real-life experiences of people and their God? Is it not the history of struggle of a particular people at particular times and places? It most certainly is.

The Word of God did not just drop from heaven outside the particularity of historical events. Our knowledge of God is not the product of an abstract philosophical and theoretical construct of the mind; it is knowledge that has developed over a long period of time in a history of humanity's involvement with God. It is in this history that humanity builds up its image and concept of God.

The question is, what is this history about? There are two ways of looking at history. Either you see history as a series of events that just happen, like natural phenomena as it were, or you understand it as a series of struggles for justice and peace in the world. The first conception of history is "accidental"; things are destined to be and just happen. Here, there are poor people and rich people. That is the way things are. Life works that way. There are servants and masters, those who have a monopoly of economic and political power and those who submit to it. Some take it further to say that this is the natural order, the way God created things. Because God made it that way, nothing can or should be done about it. All must accept their lot.

The second conception of history negates this passivity and replaces it with a struggle. Here nothing is accidental and things do not just happen. Everything is part of the struggle, either for or against the goal of securing justice. For Third World theologians, theology must be part of this building process, creating a just world and bringing in the kingdom of God. In this sense the task of the theologian is to develop theological tools to help Christians particⁱpate effectively in the struggle for justice. It is a reflection on acⁱtion in the light of faith to advance this struggle.

The next question is whether you can theologize, reflect on acⁱtion in the light of faith, without being personally involved in this struggle. The answer here is surely no. If you are not involved in this struggle, what are you involved in? The question is senseless if you believe in the first conception of history. But for the second, the question arises if you are part of the problem, on the other side of the divide, not with the Yahweh God but with Baal? Even at the simple human level, how can you have a proper understanding of a situation without being involved in it? Are you not running the risk of providing answers to the wrong questions? How can you raise the right questions about a situation in which you are not involved? Not surprisingly, the history of theology shows that it is in the height of crises—which not even theologians can escape— that new theological conceptions develop.

I agree with the Third World theologians when they say you have to be involved in historical events, in struggles between the forces of righteousness (light) and those of unrighteousness (darkness) to be able to develop an authentic theology. But this compels you to take sides. To be part of the redemptive, liberating work of God, you have no choice other than to take sides with the poor, downⁱtrodden and weak. Latin American theologians have called it an option for the poor, and this was my option when I joined the UDF.

With this option, I had to pay dearly in terms of my acceptability to those having a traditional model of theologizing and understandⁱing the work of ministry. But I nevertheless thank the Lord for the wealth of experience that I accumulated during this two-year period of direct involvement with the people. Now I can speak about what I know and what I have experienced. Now I have firsthand experiⁱence of the contradictions that are inherent in the western system of theology.

This was like an experience of incarnation for me, an experience that introduced me to the world of pain and suffering of my people. A concrete identification with the weak and oppressed in society, is, of course, a costly and risky method of witnessing. Throughout my history of struggle as a Christian, I have learned the truth of this. If you will permit me, I will speak like a fool, to use Paul's language. Six times I have been detained, at times for long periods without charge, and in three of these detentions badly tortured. I have been once charged with high treason and acquitted. My house was gasoline bombed in 1985 and I have appeared on a hit list of a death squad. When the current state of emergency was declared, I went into hiding with thousands of peace-loving South Africans for about a year. I could not go home or work from the office. I could not go to church or preach the Gospel openly. I have abandoned and restarted my studies on three separate occasions, and, in 1981, my family was evicted from the manse by my church, as I have already related.

But I thank the Lord that by passing through these experiences I have been able to develop a deeper form of spirituality which has sustained me until today. I believe in him "who is greater than anyone in this world" (1 John 4:4). For this reason "they will never be lost and no one will ever pluck them from my hand" (John 10:27). I believe that he who has started the good work in us will sustain it until the end.

To those who have taken the Word of God seriously, none of these experiences should come as a surprise. Were not the prophets of old detained or killed? Was Jesus not cruelly crucified? Do we not read of the apostles being harassed, imprisoned and even killed? Do we not talk of the *martyria,* the blood witness in the early Church? Do we not read about the apostles who were scattered and exiled from Jerusalem and yet continued witnessing in other territories? Don't we read of David going into hiding and living underground? Why are we then so surprised? Do we not read in the Bible that we perceive God's love precisely in that he laid down his life for us? Are we not called to do likewise for our brethren? (1 John 3:16)

Criminals, Communists
and Christians

Both in my struggle to be Christian and my involvement in the liberation movement in South Africa, I have been struck by the way anti-Communist propaganda is used to turn any critique of the apartheid system into a criminal activity. The 1950 Communism Act was deliberately made broad in scope to include any person who resisted, criticized or acted against the apartheid regime. This crude approach of the Nationalist Government, which directly reflected the McCarthy era in the USA, bundled both so-called Communists and all other democrats together in an alliance that haunts both the west and white South Africa today.

The biggest mistake of the South African intelligence forces, like those of most key western countries, is to use anti-Communist propaganda to try to suppress the oppressed and make them accept their oppression indefinitely. In fact, South Africa and its western allies have contributed greatly to the international renown of the east through this crude propaganda. There are two reasons why the impact on the west and on white South Africa is different from the reaction of the Third World. The first is that blacks in South Africa, as in most Third World Countries, have never been part of east-west ideological conflict and the related Cold War. We do not share the same obsession with the issue as most westerners and white South Africans. Indeed, Third World people have often found in practice better allies in the east in their struggles for liberation and independence than in the west.

The second reason is that the people who try to sell this propaganda are the very oppressors, those responsible for the exploitation of the black masses in this country. The proponents of the propaganda are the beneficiaries of the system. The propaganda leaflets about Communists and countries in the east, with their details of torture and killings, in fact highlighted for me the way these methods were daily used by the South African security forces. I am a living witness of what the South African security forces do to political detainees. Most of the things they said Communists do, they did to me. My concrete knowledge of an evil, satanic system therefore is the racist system of South Africa. For me it is not Communists who are the problem but these Christians who oppress us, exploit us, detain us and torture us even unto death. And here I am speaking for countless blacks in South Africa.

The contradiction we face has been well expressed in the booklet *Evangelical Witness in South Africa.** We have been dispossessed of our land, have been dehumanized, discriminated against and exploited by people who claim to be Christian. To deepen our dilemma, those western countries which most lay claim to a western Christian heritage support them and reinforce their capacity to retain white power. On the other hand, the Communist countries have shown themselves willing to assist us to be freed from the apartheid system.

Nelson Mandela's answer in court to the question of his organization's alliance with the Communists illuminates the point that I am making. He told the court that Communists were the first white people who were prepared to drink tea with him and sit for a meal around the same table, in stark contrast to his fellow-Christian white South Africans.

I believe that the real contradiction and dilemma of whites in South Africa and in the west is that they happen historically to be the colonizers. So when the colonized subjects revolt against the colonial power or against neocolonialism, they are pitted against western powers or, in this case, against South Africa's racist regime. Whenever the colonized of the Third World sought assistance, with few exceptions, they found it only in the east. This is the pitfall of the western tradition, this placing of short-term self-interest before justice, of their economic and strategic security interests above the demands of justice. It hardly needs saying that this policy is simply contrary to the demands of the Gospel.

Maybe this is the dilemma of all systems whose intrinsic design

*Johannesburg: "Concerned Evangelicals," 1986.

is meant to serve the interest of the few rich and powerful in society and whose ideology is one of domination and exploitation. If you create an apartheid system designed to serve the interests of the 15 percent of the population who are privileged and white, plus a negligible percentage of privileged blacks, then you are bound to face the reaction, resistance and revolt of the marginalized millions who happen to be mostly black. If you create an economic system which benefits a few at the expense of the majority of South Africans, then you must be prepared to be challenged by the victims at the bottom of the pyramid. All forms of propaganda attempting to justify this unjust system prove counterproductive and work against their own goals.

The international dimension of unjust and oppressive systems geared to serve the interests of the rich and powerful nations is also worth reflecting on. The west, or the business community, tends to support even tyrannical regimes, particularly in the Third World, provided they maintain the necessary stability for them to continue to make their profit and insure the so-called national security interests of the rich and powerful nations. This, in most instances, is done at the expense of millions of lives in the Third World. It is done irrespective of the enormous pain, suffering and misery it causes countless victims of these sophisticated systems. Here, morality or the question of justice does not arise. In the final analysis, it seems that morality and the generation of profit and the satisfaction of security interests are simply not compatible.

The point I am making here was clarified by an important businessman in South Africa who, when his company was challenged to act justly, said, "If as a director I began to act for moral reasons at the expense of company profits, I would lose my job immediately." The contradictions of the system were rooted so deeply in it that such people were free only to lose their job. One industrial relations officer of a big company was frank enough to tell me that his job was to manage the inherent conflict within the system and to make this conflict as manageable as possible. No amount of propaganda to buttress the system can disguise this reality; the success of the South African government's efforts in this regard is either nonexistent or so short-lived as to be inconsequential for blacks, despite the millions of dollars spent on it, the vast resources and number of people dedicated to its success.

To seek peace without overcoming this contradiction is doomed to failure. The Gospel is very clear on the matter. It declares that there can be no peace without justice as a basic truth. If justice and honesty come to dominate our lives then, and only then, will peace be sure. This is our vision of the kingdom of God and we know that there is no easy path into it. Listen to what Jesus said: "If any man would come after me, let him deny himself and take up his cross and follow me. For whoever would save his life will lose it, and whoever loses his life for my sake, he will save it. For what does it profit a man if he gains the whole world and loses or forfeits himself?" (Luke 9:23–25).

The refusal to heed this Gospel truth threatens to lead us all toward total destruction. The letter of James says: "What causes wars, and what causes fighting amongst you? Is it not your passions that you are at war in your members? You desire and do not have, so you kill. And you covet and cannot obtain, so you fight and wage war . . . God opposes the proud, but gives grace to the humble" (James 4:1–6).

On Saving the First and Second Worlds

My understanding of the role of Third World Christians in relation to the whole global conflict has developed through travel. Between September 1986 and March 1987 I passed through two frontline states and traveled to nine countries in Europe plus the USA. and Canada. I was able to reflect on the experience at the second general assembly of EATWOT (the Ecumenical Association of Third World Theologians) in Oaxtepec, Mexico. After an earlier visit to Europe in March–April 1986, I wrote a letter to the friends and partners I had met, reflecting on what I had seen and heard. The conclusion of this letter was that the pain, oppression and suffering of people in the Third World were somehow directly or indirectly linked to the prosperity and luxury of this other world. In the universal Church of Christ, the south-north contradiction was basic to us all.

In searching for the nature of the north-south linkage, I found it necessary to invent the terms "primary" and "secondary" sin. I felt that the Church always tends to address itself to the manifestations of secondary sin rather than primary sin. Because of the very sophistication of humanity in a sinful form of life, this primary sin eludes the analysis of the Church. For example, the Church highlights the sinfulness of people who steal from their bosses without addressing the sin of those who cause them to be poor by exploiting them at work in the first place. The primary sinner parades in acceptable apparel and looks very respectable in church; they are dignified people. You will not find the pastor lambasting this class of people in a congregation; the sermon will be about the sin of the poor and the weak.

During my second visit, I heard more and more about the fear of those in the west about the east. My impression in West Germany was that this was more of an obsession than an ordinary fear. I could understand, however, that this fear of Communism was fanned by the proximity of East Germany and the tension of division in Berlin between east and west. Some people felt the pain personally and had relatives on each side of the wall who were close to them.

But the danger here is that people could become so obsessed with the fear of Communism that they could completely fail to listen to or hear God speaking to them. They become so blinded by this fear that no matter how cruel the act, it is justified in the fight against Communism. These are the roots of slogans such as "Kill a Commie for Jesus" that were common during the Vietnam war. Once people are taught to believe that Communist forces are behind liberation movements in the Third World, they become willing to support any regime, however corrupt and unjust, to retain power. So today some sincerely think, "Rather apartheid than Communism," and help keep the apartheid system rather than risk a "Communist takeover." And they would justify this position morally in terms of the lesser of two evils.

On the other hand, some of the countries in the east have been so obsessed with the counter-revolutionary nature of religion that they are tempted to fight any form of religious expression as part of their program to defend their revolution and form of government. But, of course, they also have a basis for this attitude. The fact of the matter is that Christianity, in particular, has been an instrument in counter-revolutionary strategies used by most western countries against the resistance movements of the Third World or against the socialist countries of the east. In their efforts to turn religious people against the expanding influence of socialism in the world, they use Marx's dictums on religion out of context and blow them out of proportion in order to create a religious counter-revolutionary force. Conservatives in the west treat Marx's approach to religion as if it were a central part of his philosophy, the very heart of Communism, the only "gospel" he ever preached in his life.

Fidel Castro, in his conversations with Frei Betto,* explains why Christians are discriminated against as far as membership of the party is concerned. He describes how "the wealthy class had a

---

Fidel & Religion (Simon and Schuster, New York: 1986).

monopoly on the Church; it tried to use it and to lead bishops, priests and ordinary Catholics to take counter-revolutionary positions.'' In another part of the same book, he says, ''All the privileged classes that had a monopoly on the Church were against the revolution, so when in organizing the party we excluded those who believed in God, we were excluding them as potential counter-revolutionaries, not as Catholics.'' He goes on to claim that ''if the masses in our country—the great masses of workers, farmers and university students—had been active Christians, we could not have formed a revolutionary party based on those principles. But since most of the active Catholics were well-to-do, supported the counter-revolution, and left the country,'' he says, ''we could—and had to—establish a severe, orthodox rule.''

If the two extreme positions persist—the violent anti-Communist activity of the west in defense of the rich and powerful oppressors in the world and the dogmatic Marxist position that opposes any expression of religion as counter-revolutionary—it is clear there can be no end to the cold war and no peace. While this east-west conflict continues, we are all but a nuclear button away from total destruction, a position felt most keenly by Europeans. Even after the positive steps that have been taken in nuclear disarmament recently, we all live under the shadow of annihilation every minute of our lives.

Joe Holland describes this situation as a cultural ''crisis of all industrial civilization.'' In the preface to the enlarged and revised edition of *Social Analysis, Linking Faith and Justice* (Orbis: 1983), written with Pete Henriot, there is the following important insight: ''The classical secular left has rightly perceived the great drive towards social destruction at the heart of modern civilization. But it has generally failed to perceive the destructive blocking of divine creativity, which flows from an ever-deepening progressive secularization of society.'' They go on to say: ''The classical left thus challenges social destruction but cuts itself off from the religious root of creativity.''

For the classical religious right, the problem is secularization. It sees the ''progressive'' movement as deepening this process of secularization. But this religious right, say Holland and Henriot, ''fails to understand the prophetic side of the divine and ends up defending the very social destruction that the Left fights against.'' ''The

Right tries to retrieve an authoritarian, patriarchal, militaristic society, tied this time to powerful modern technology. It appeals to a divine image,'' they say, ''but that divine image is no longer the living God of justice and peace. It is rather a war god, a god of oppression, an idol. This idol in turn provides religious legitimation for demonic destruction.'' Their conclusion is that the other ''two worlds'' are entering into a ''negative convergence in the single social and spiritual crisis of industrial civilisation.'' Ironically, both are struggling to shape the destiny of the Third World, where new signs of a social and spiritual creativity, which transcend and defy the destructive tendencies in both, are emerging.

This reality has led me to believe that the only people who can save the world today are the victims of this scramble for power and influence. These are the poor people of the Third World. I believe that it is in their poverty and weakness that they will save both the first and second worlds. Third World theologians have already established this premise and are acting on it. Hugo Assman, for example, speaks of the ''epistemological privilege of the poor.'' What does he mean? He is merely arguing that the way the poor see the world is closer to the world's reality than the way the rich see it. Indeed you can take this argument further to say that the poor have an hermeneutical key to the depth of the truths contained in the Bible.

There is a text in the Bible that dramatizes this reality—truth—succinctly. After Jesus had appointed seventy-two disciples to go preaching, they returned rejoicing. ''Lord,'' they said, ''even the demons submit to us when we use your name.'' ''Yes,'' he replied, ''I have given you power to tread underfoot serpents and scorpions and the whole strength of the enemy; nothing shall ever hurt you. Yet do not rejoice that the spirits submit to you; rejoice rather that your names are written in heaven.'' Then comes Jesus' joyful prayer: ''I bless you, Father, Lord of heaven and earth, for hiding these things from the learned and the clever and revealing them to mere children. Yes, Father, for that is what it pleased you to do'' (Luke 10:17–21).

Thinking about My Family—
Thinking about the Kingdom

If I were asked if I would have liked to live the type of life I am living now, I would most certainly have said no. If I were asked to choose a particular type or form of life to live, I would have definitely chosen to live a normal life like other people. But now I am living a life that is not my own; I am living not for myself but for others. I am living a life full of risks and uncertainties, to such a degree that I work on the basis that I could be assassinated at any time of my life. It is a life of detentions, torture and treason trial, but no crime, even within the very unjust apartheid laws.

It is a life full of external pressures that disrupt any form of normal family life. My family sees very little of me. My wife, Kagiso, has assumed almost all the burdens of the family. She always has to act like a single-parent mother. Our boys, Obakeng and Otlile, will be eight and four by the end of 1988. Even when I am not in prison or in hiding, they see very little of me. The family knows very little of a Daddy who goes out with them—except on work trips.

When I am faced with a situation where I am constrained, because of my faith and my understanding of my calling, to lay down my life or risk it for others, I also put their lives on the firing line. I often say that at least my dear wife, Kagiso, made a conscious decision to get married to me knowing the possible consequences of the type of ministry I was involved in, but the poor kids had no chance at all to make a choice. And when our house was attacked with three gasoline bombs and caught fire with Otlile (then only eight months old) almost engulfed by the flames, I began to realize that the poor kids were victims of circumstances beyond their control.

So I am not "of my family." Maybe because I consider them as

68

part of myself and cannot see them as people outside myself.

Having said all this, I want to thank God for having given me the type of family I have, particularly my wife, Kagiso. I doubt that without her I would have been the same person. She is of course no saint, just as I am no saint, like any other person. She has normal human concerns about the family, my safety, and the type of life we are living.

I remember during 1984 Kagiso went through her worst experience when she was due to give birth to Otlile in the heat of the campaign against the new South African apartheid constitution. I was not there when she desperately needed me. The night of Otlile's birth I was called at 9:00 P.M. to deal with an emergency in another family whose father was one of the many who were in preventative detention under Section 28 of the Internal Security Act. During my absence, one hour and a half after I had left, Otlile also called, announcing that he would be landing in this world any moment. Our nextdoor neighbor was called to come and help Kagiso. At about eleven o'clock I arrived and found her gone. I felt guilty and angry with myself, but without any answer to the problem. The only thing to do was race to the maternity clinic. There I was delayed putting on the right attire to enter the delivery ward. As I entered the ward and embraced Kagiso, Otlile landed.

"Otlile" is an unusual name I had not heard of myself. But it is the name I conceived while racing to the clinic and pronounced after that cry which announced the arrival of the baby. The name means "he has arrived" or "he has come." Besides the fact that the child had come irrespective of all the problems and complexities of our family life, there were two other meanings in my mind as I coined the name. The first had to do with our type of life. I was due to run a Black Theology conference at St. Francis Xavier's, Cape Town, as general secretary of the Institute for Contextual Theology (ICT) from September 10–14, 1984. I could not easily pull out of it, and I was scared the baby would come during the conference. I therefore prayed that the baby would come before the conference, and indeed he came.

The other meaning is more difficult to translate into English because of the English language's sexist gender connotations. "Otlile" means "God has come."* It is interesting that most African lan-

---

*Literally, "He/She has come."

Kagiso Chikane: *"She has assumed almost all the burdens of the family."*

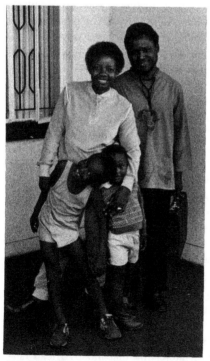

Chikane with his wife, Kagiso, and children, Otlile ("He has arrived") and Obakeng ("Praise God"), at their home in Soweto.

JOYCE HOLLYDAY

The Apostolic Faith Mission of Africa

Tel: 44-9637 (Office)

P.O. Box 23420
INNESDALE
0031

30th October, 1981

Pastor F. Chikane
P.O. Box 65
KAGISO
1744

REGISTERED MAIL

Dear Pastor Chikane

RE: SUSPENSION FROM FULL-TIME SERVICE

I refer to my letter dated 4th September, 1981 and the Executive Council
Meetings which were held on 20th and 28th October, 1981.

The following decision was taken:

"In view of the fact that Pastor Frank Chikane did not keep the promise
he made regarding the conditions of his ordination, and because this Council
finds that there is no change in his attitude; he be suspended from full-time
ministry for 12 months from 28th October, 1981, in the hope that there will
be a change of heart."

Yours in His Service

G.S. ERASMUS
GENERAL SECRETARY

Copies sent to: 1. West Rand District
2. The Missions Director

Frank Chikane at the launch of the United Democratic Front's "Unban the ANC" campaign in 1986.

Chikane delivers the first Bishop Ambrose Reeves Memorial Lecture at Westminster Central Hall, London, in April 1988. Reeves was the first of a succession of church leaders who stood out against apartheid.

ABEL LAGOS

In February 1988, church leaders confront the state to protest banning of anti-apartheid organizations: marching on parliament are (from left to right), Archbishop Stephen Naidoo, Archbishop Desmond Tutu (Roman Catholic and Anglican Archbishops of Cape Town), Rev. Allan Boesak, and Frank Chikane. All were arrested.

Exclusion Order from Namibia

NOTICE TO:

PASTOR FRANK CHIKANE

Whereas the Cabinet has reason to believe that your presence is likely to endanger the security of South West Africa / Namibia or its inhabitants or the maintenance of public order and or will engender or is likely to engender a feeling of hostility between members of the different population groups, you are hereby prohibited in terms of section 9 of the Residence of certain persons in South West Africa Regulation Act, 1985 (Act 33 of 1985) to be in South West Africa / Namibia.

.....Y. del k=th......
CHAIRMAN OF THE CABINET
(By order of the Cabinet)

DATE: 22-05-1986

"We are punished in a so-called Christian country, simply for being engaged in church work." Chikane stands outside the bombed wreckage of Khotso House, headquarters of the South African Council of Churches in Johannesburg.

guages do not have a gender problem in referring to God. In these languages, God has no gender. As Gabriel Setiloane says, in the Tswana language God is neither male nor female, but God. To us therefore, God had visited us. God was in our midst in time of need, God was present with us (Emmanuel), and gave us the baby. Otlile's second name is Lehlohonolo, which means "a blessing."

The name of our first child is Obakeng, which means "praise God," or literally, "praise him/her." The second name, which his mother does not like, reflects the beginning of the struggle in the family, and is Aluta. It comes from the slogan *"A luta continua."* Obakeng was born just after my third detention in 1980, and to me life presented itself as a life of struggles between justice and injustice, between God and the devil, between good and evil, between the gospel of truth and the gospel of the oppressive forces of our time. Kagiso did not like the name because she did not like the way it was a constant reminder of our type of life. She also did not like the name because of a Setswana saying. She said to me, "You know, the Setswana saying, *'Leina le ya boreelong,'* might just become true; that is, the meaning of the name you give to a child could be fulfilled in the child's life."

But what is special about my wife, Kagiso? What is unique about her that she has kept the family together and intact, so much so that we can say, "Thank God we are still married"? I have talked about this unique aspect of her character to other people, to friends, but I have not told her of it. She is going to see it for the first time when she reads this manuscript.

She is human like any other human being. She gets hurt and feels pain; she reacts like any human being. Yet she is an understanding partner. If this were not the case, our marriage would be no more. The difficulty, of course, is trying to reconcile being human and being understanding in our situation. This conflict manifested itself in 1984 when Kagiso expressed her concern about my ministry and my involvement with those victims of apartheid who were engaged in a struggle to bring our pain to an end. She realized that I was working myself right into detention or death and that by challenging this evil, racist system of South Africa I was inviting it to land brutally on me. Listen to what she said: "Although I understand what you are doing, that it is part and parcel of your ministry and calling, I am concerned about your life. Even if I understand that

with this type of ministry, which challenges the powerful oppressors in the name of the Lord, you will land up in detention, maybe
tortured and even killed, I also love you. I would not like to see
you in that situation. But I cannot stop you. I understand. . . .''

The unique thing about her is that although she expresses her
concerns and her frustrations about me, once the enemy has struck
in the form of detention, charges for treason and attacking the family, she switches on to a new wavelength and confronts the reality
with determination, confidence and a level of understanding that
intrigues me. You could say that when she is faced with the worst
she takes the bull by the horns. In Sesotho we would say: *Mme o
tshwara thipa ka bohaleng* (''Mother holds the knife on the sharp
side'').

In fact, it is during times like these, when I am frustrated and
down, that she becomes an encouragement and does her best to lift
me up. At times the sudden shift is just unreal to me, yet it is real;
it happens and it works. It happened during my fourth and longest
detention, from November 1981 to July 1982, which came immediately after I had been suspended by my church, the Apostolic
Faith Mission, from October 1981 to September 1982. They suspended me because they said I was involved in politics, because I
had appeared in the press. Their argument was that because I was
appearing in the press, critically attacking the apartheid system, I
was embarrassing the church. They gave us two months after the
date of suspension to vacate the manse, or mission house, as people
call it in the townships. We had to find our own accommodation.
They wanted another pastor to take over the congregation.

Before we found alternative accommodation—a difficult task, as
you would expect in a country where you had thousands of black
family units on a waiting list for housing while there was plenty for
whites—I was detained. Instead of worrying about my detention
and the welfare of my family, the church concerned itself solely
about when the family was going to leave the manse. When they
had failed to leave the house on the different dates given to the
family, finally a six-man delegation of senior pastors was sent to
give Kagiso a final warning to leave. When she said that she had
not been able to find alternative accommodation, she was told that
was not their business.

''When your husband did what he did,'' they said, ''he must

have been aware of the consequences thereof. But he is clever anyway, and he must solve this problem.'' Even when I am in detention! My wife was never as hurt by the church and by Christians as she was that day, she told me. It is a miracle that she remained a Christian. But within days of this ultimatum, members of the greater Body of Christ and friends came to her rescue and she found herself a house in Soweto.

It was during this experience that she demonstrated her extraordinary character and faced the challenge head-on. The same happened when I was detained in February 1985 and charged with high treason. When I was released on bail in May 1985 and subjected to restrictions amounting to house arrest, our house was attacked and, a week later, a hit list was discovered where my name appeared with thirteen other community leaders (among whom were Archbishop Desmond Tutu and Father Lebamang Sebidi). She said that they were not going to leave me alone to stay elsewhere—I could not, of course, move like the others to avoid the assassins, because of my restrictions. She was prepared to stand by me until death do part us.

The question at the beginning was whether I would have chosen this type of life had I been given a choice, and I said no. But this has not just been a question people have asked me. It's a question that I have asked myself from time to time when we faced those difficult situations which, in almost all cases, were out of our control. Although we were aware of the possible consequences of my type of ministry, it became clearer to us during 1986 that we would never lead a normal life like other families in this world. I remember Kagiso articulating this position very clearly one day. We realized that I could not stay at home with them, nor could I work in my office at ICT, because of a possible detention under the state of emergency regulations and the possibility of being assassinated or kidnapped by the rampant death squads organized by agents of the apartheid system. I could not even go to church and continue with my ministry, although, ironically, I became available to those who were in hiding.

It seems that as long as this apartheid system exists we shall not be able to live a normal life as a family. This is a shattering experience for us and the children. Do we have a way out? I doubt it. In fact Jesus tried to find a way out. At the Mount of Olives, as

Luke calls it, at Gethsemane according to Matthew, faced with the death of the Cross, he became sorrowful and troubled, even to death. Because of this he prayed that this cup pass (Matthew 22:36–46) or be removed from him (Luke 22:39–46). But, he said, not my will but your will be done. No one, no human being, really wants to go the way of the Cross, to suffer and die. Not even Jesus!

But, given our calling to proclaim the kingdom of God in this world, it seems as if there is no chance of surviving in the face of the evil powers that be, which are threatened by the reign of God in this world. They fear this message we are proclaiming, and the message proclaimed through the struggle and victory of Third World peoples. If the kingdom of God comes, they will have no one to oppress, no one to exploit—especially economically to make their profits—so they can live in luxury at the expense of the poor, weak and powerless; no one to dominate, no one to undermine or humiliate, no one to dehumanize. Yes, there will be no place for blatant white racism or apartheid. Those who live at the expense of the blood, life and sweat of others fear even the mention of a classless society that could be compatible with the ideals of the kingdom. They are afraid of life in a world where righteousness and justice reign, a world that is emptied like a vacuum of its sin.

The problem is that they could be vacuumed up with all the sin. This is what Jesus really meant when he said that they will not enter the kingdom of God. Because Jesus must reign until all his enemies have been put under his feet. And then comes the end when he will deliver the kingdom to God, his Father, after destroying every rule and every authority and power, so that God may be everything to everyone (1 Corinthians 15:24–28). When I read some of these passages of scripture, I begin to understand why we are charged with treason for preaching the Gospel, for this is treasonable stuff.

The point I want to make is that "until now the kingdom of heaven has suffered violence, and men of violence take it by force" (Matthew 11:12). It is for this reason that Jesus died: because he challenged those violent forces who wanted to take this kingdom by force. He claimed the kingdom as rightfully belonging to his Father, and he was crucified for it.

One United States theologian remarked at the Kairos Convocation in Chicago, where I was a guest speaker, that he does not believe that Jesus came to die as the Church would like us to believe. *He simply had no choice but to die,* given the evil nature of his society. I understand what this theologian was trying to say. The message is that if we Christians could begin to proclaim the kingdom as Jesus did in the face of all these evil, powerful systems and empires of the world, *we have no choice but to die.*

Although this is a ghastly reality, maybe it has to happen to the Church so that it can come down from the places of power where it was put by Constantine fourteen centuries ago. The Church, to be Church in the world today, must reject the dominant ideology of the powerful and take the way of the Cross. This, of course, will mean that it will have to take the side of the weak, poor and powerless in the world. Once this is done in opposition to the sinful ideology of the dominant classes in society, then the Church is bound to be persecuted like the Church of the Apostles, John, Peter and Paul. Witnessing, which today is a comfortable mission for many, will become "blood witnessing": martyrdom.

But we need to thank God that Jesus rose again and is alive. This assures us that in our death a new life will rise, a new society, a new heaven and a new earth (Revelation 21). Philippians 1:20–21 became a reality for me on the fourth floor of Krugersdorp Police Station. I was tortured there and made to stand for fifty hours with teams of interrogators working eight hours per shift during my 1977–1978 detention. When one of my torturers told me that I was "going to die slowly but sure," I said to him that "for me to live is Christ but to die is gain." I told him that if he let me live I would still continue even more vehemently to proclaim the Gospel and challenge the evil and satanic system of apartheid. But if they let me die, then it would be gain for me, because I would be with the Lord. Because then and now, as always, Christ will be honored in my body whether by life or by death. Whichever way, their kingdom of apartheid will come to an end and Jesus will reign.

Letter to the Churches
in Europe: April 1986

TO ALL THE CHURCHES/CHRISTIANS IN EUROPE AND ICT
PARTNERS IN THE STRUGGLE FOR A RELEVANT THEOL-
OGY ON THE STRUGGLE FOR JUSTICE IN SA

Dear Brothers and Sisters,

We are about to touch down at Jan Smuts Airport in Johannesburg after an extensive visit from March 10 to April 4, 1986. This
mission in Europe covered seven countries: the UK, Sweden, Holland, Belgium, France, West Germany and Switzerland. Unfortu-
nately, time did not allow me to visit Norway, Finland, Denmark,
Portugal, Spain, Italy and other countries in Europe. The program
in these countries involved meetings (discussions) with the Institute's partners, foreign and international offices of the churches in
these countries, councils of churches, the World Council of Churches
(WCC) and various other relevant church groups. The program also
involved contacts and meetings with anti-apartheid groups, the ECC,
Socialist groups of the European Parliament, Socialist Democratic
Parties in Europe, the foreign ministry of Sweden and an official of
the foreign office in Switzerland. I also attended a meeting between
church leaders and bankers in Hamburg where the question of loans
to the apartheid regime was discussed.

The last two weeks before my departure to undertake this mission were the most difficult. They were clouded with the possibility
of being stopped from leaving the country by the apartheid regime.
It was difficult because it meant preparing for a mission without
being sure that it would be carried out at the end. The high level
of uncertainty was disturbing indeed. It was difficult to forget the
bitter experience of 1985 when I was detained eight days before I

could leave for this same mission. A whole month's program had to be canceled while my life was wasted in an apartheid dungeon.

When P.W. Botha announced that the State of Emergency would be lifted on Friday, March 7, 1986, just two days before my departure, we had more courage to complete the preparations hastily, as there was a higher probability that they would not interfere with me and mess up the gains they wanted to score internationally. On the day of departure my family followed me around a transparent glass wall at the airport to make sure I had gone through all the control gates, especially the passport control. Only after takeoff did I feel a bit safe from the harassment and brutality of the apartheid system. I felt I had taken off from hell on an Alitalia ticket.

We landed at Rome airport the morning of March 10, 1986 in transit to the United Kingdom. While following the transit signs I was approached by a very unfriendly man who later declared himself to be a policeman. He demanded to search my baggage. While he was busy with my baggage, I observed that his colleagues were stopping any person who looked like a non-European or from Africa and the Middle East—maybe all those who came from the Third World. I did not know! But what became clear to me was that there was a clear demarcation between the rich, powerful oppressors and exploiters, and the poor, weak, oppressed and exploited millions of this world. It became clear that I had just moved from the fire into the frying pan to be "fried" in a more "civilized" way. I realized that I had actually not taken off from hell to safety but to an internationalized dimension of our brutality and oppression.

We touched down at Heathrow Airport just before midday, and the three days I spent in London just confirmed my feelings at Rome. It became clear that the actual people who were responsible for our oppression are outside our country. Although there are many groups engaged in different awareness programs, campaigns and protests, the majority of British citizens are blind to the sin of our exploitation and oppression. They are not aware that they are responsible for our pain, suffering and even death. When we are killed they sympathize with us and blame apartheid, but they are not aware that in fact they are responsible for this death and destruction in our country and that apartheid is just a local smoke screen to soothe their consciences.

If the British people were not blind, Britain would not veto all resolutions against the apartheid regime. If the British community was not blind, they could not allow Margaret Thatcher to continue for another day longer. Well, maybe we have to go through this pain and suffering, maybe we need to die for the redemption of British society. Maybe our blood and our broken bodies will be their salvation. It looks as if our fight for liberation is going to be a fight to liberate the western countries who are responsible for our oppression. I pray to God that we be given the power and the courage to drink of the cup of Jesus, the cup of suffering, for the sake of many.

After going through the other European countries, I was convinced that the fundamental problem in the West is that what I call the "primary sin" in the world has eluded the Church. As a result, the Church is obsessed with the "secondary sin" of the victims of the primary sinners. It should not be forgotten that mission in the Third World happened at the same time as the process of colonization and exploitation of the Third World's resources, raw materials, etc., which over the years created the gross disparities between the north and the south. The process of industrialization in these areas resulted in the worsening of the already unjust relations between those whose only survival was the selling of their labor. Mission activity therefore shifted its focus to deal with the response of Third World peoples to this gross injustice.

Because of the increasing sophistication of this system of economic injustice and the modern justification of brutal forms of human relations (racist, classist, sexist) the missionaries (Church), with their primitive theological tools, could no longer detect the primary sin. With their outdated methods of social analysis (if they engaged in any analysis at all), this sophisticated and subtle serpent simply eluded them and tricked them into spending all their time, energy and resources flogging the wrong horse.

This is what I call the "secondary sin." Just go through the sermons of the last three to five centuries. They hammer at the "thieves," "adulterers," "murderers," "drunkards," etc. These to me are secondary sinners. The primary sinners are those who turned them into thieves by robbing them of their resources, energy, time and labor (surplus labor). The primary sinners are those who invest in South Africa, who support their market and give loans to this evil apartheid system to allow the tiny white minority to use these resources to hold power and maintain this brutal system at the expense of hundreds of thousands of lives. The primary sinners are those who benefit from and draw profits out of apartheid at the expense of the pain and suffering of the black masses in South Africa. They maintain and enjoy standards of living in Europe that are built on a deliberate policy and system of impoverishment of the Third World. I believe now that if sermons or missions in Europe are to mean anything at all, are to be a real *"Missio Dei,"* they must focus on this primary sin of the modern, so-called civilized, world.

This is not directed to the European scene only. It also applies to their Third World partners, and in particular their South African partners, in this sin: the multinationals, business people, large co-operatives and the apartheid regime. It applies to the recipients of investments, those on the spot who exploit the raw materials and other resources at the expense of the local populace and market them to their partners overseas for their benefit. It applies to the beneficiaries of bank loans, those who benefit out of the economic prop-up of the apartheid system to lengthen its life span. Thus the churches in South Africa and in other parts of the Third World, the south, have the same responsibility to the churches in the north. They must begin to focus their sermons on these "dignified," high-class, "civilized" sinners.

The story of the so-called adulterous woman in John 8:1–11 captures this problem in a simple but sharp way. Jesus dealt with those powerful and protected scribes and Pharisees by saying: "Let him who is without sin among you be the first to throw a stone at her." Confronted with this reflection on their own primary sin which exposed their hypocrisy, "they went away." After having dealt with this primary sin, Jesus turned to the woman and said to her, "Go and do not sin again" (v. 11).

Maybe I am wrong to say that this sin has eluded the Church. The reality of the matter might be that the Church deliberately closed its eyes to it because of the enormous self-interests of the participants in this mission of the Church and the need for the Church to serve the interests of this class of people in society. Doesn't the Church benefit from this whole system of injustice in the world? Is the Church not sustained financially and materially by these systems and persons? Faced with this reality, has the Church any ability to free itself from this Babylonian captivity? Can the Church be part of the whole liberation struggle, the struggle for new liberated systems, structures and relationships between those who are actors in these systems?

So much for primary and secondary sins, for lack of better terminology. Even language has been appropriated by the powerful in society to serve their interests.

This brings us to an expression quoted by one of the participants at a workshop on the Kairos Document held in Zürich, Switzerland, in the process of grappling with the *kairos* of the western church, of western Christians. The statement was expressed in the following way: our problem is that we are stuck with love and charity in our response to the evils of this world rather than justice. We in the West are compelled by love, Christian love and concern about the brutality of some of the systems in the Third World, we are moved by the hunger and poverty to give charity. But we never go beyond charity to justice.

The implications of this statement became very clear to the group. Giving charity was seen as necessary to save lives in these devastated areas of oppression and exploitation and to alleviate pain and suffering. But it was noted that this good generous activity on its own cannot resolve the fundamental problem. It remains an "ambulance ministry" to help save the victims of a vicious system. To participate in the ministry of addressing the fundamental problem, Christians in the West must engage in the struggle to uproot the foundations of this problem, which are mainly based in their countries. They must have a deliberate program of action as part of their confession and their commitment to the Gospel. To put it in crude terms, terms that are threatening to some people, they too must engage in a liberation struggle to redeem and free themselves of this subtle system which benefits them, directly or indirectly making them partners in this primary sin.

Churches need to begin to challenge the bankers at their home base. They need to challenge businesspeople, corporations, governments and parastate institutions at their home base. They need to challenge their membership and raise their consciousness about this sin and equip them with better, more critical theological tools to detect it. Christians and committed people at the grass-roots level also need to undertake campaigns to mobilize their people to deal with this problem from below. It seems to me that this is going to become increasingly the most effective way of expressing solidarity in action and struggle, rather than necessarily stopping the attack of apartheid at the frontline of the battle ground (South Africa itself). Our solidarity, our sharing of the same body of Christ, our ecumenism, will be expressed in this common action of faith on all fronts of this war (struggle) against evil and injustice in the world. Our unity in Christ can only be unity in action, united action in struggle; it cannot be a unity that leaves the very structures of oppression intact.

The 1981 theme of the CCFD (Comité Catholique Contre la Faim pour le Développement) based in France struck me in its definition of solidarity. Their theme was solidarity, and their definition of this theme was: "Nothing will ever change in the Third World if nothing changes here."

In expanding on this theme they said that "nothing will ever change in our world, in the Third World, if nothing changes in your world, in your societies, in the international structures of domination and profit whose centers of power are located in your countries." The appeal of the 1971 Roman Synod of Bishops, as referred to in one of CCFD's 1981 pamphlets, is also helpful in this regard: "Action on behalf of justice and participation in the transformation of the world fully appear to us as a constitutive dimension of the preaching of the gospel, or, in other words, of the Church's mission for the redemption of the human race and its liberation from every oppressive situation."

This "transformation of the world," this redemption of the "human race," this "liberation from every oppressive situation" requires the setting up of new structures and new systems to encourage a just redistribution of wealth, power and knowledge to close the gap between the rich and the poor, between the north and the south. It means discovering the causes of underdevelopment, injustices and inequalities. It means getting involved in "preventative solidarity."

This type of solidarity requires a profound change in the way people think, in the whole conception of life. It means destroying the Baals of today that have been handed on to us by our respected traditions and given good names like "Christian western culture" or "civilization." These are the false gods of egoism, individualism, self-interest, exploitation and excess, consumerism, elitism, etc.—the false god of anti-Communism that justifies torture and causes pain and suffering and the brutal killing of innocent people by the thousands.

Bishop Sastre is quoted in the same CCFD pamphlet as saying: ". . . this liberation is not possible unless the veil of egoism falls from our hearts." He continues: "The real issue in the battle is to reveal the features in human beings which make them most human, to restore to them their dignity of being, in the image and likeness of God."

The demand, therefore, is to change our ways of thinking, acting and living. It means changing our attitude to life, our values and priorities. This radical change must happen in us as individuals, as social groups, as nations and in the whole international community and in international relations. This sends us back to that old Christian concept of "conversion" as expressed by Christ and his apostles. The word has been subverted by the Church over the centuries. It sends us to the radical change Paul and other apostles talked about: the new creature, the creation of a new humanity, a new cosmos where the old has passed away and the new has come (2 Corinthians 5:17).

This whole new reality and new way of thinking means that we must redefine our concept of partnership. We know from Church history that it took more than half a century for the Church to redefine its concept of mission because of pressure from below, from the Third World. Mission went through its *kairos* from the early part of this century to the seventies. We are now going through another *kairos* in our very new concept of partnership, which replaced the old imperialistic, paternalistic, missionary form of relationship.

In the editorial of the January–March 1986 issues of *Christian Aid News*, it is said that "Christian Aid needs to continue to challenge the insularity which often creeps into generosity." The editorial continues to say that "The agency is more than a channel for funds: it should provide the wave length for a *'reverse image'* of the Third World" (my emphasis). Two crucial issues are raised here:

1. The need to "challenge the insularity which often creeps into generosity," and

2. The need to "provide the wavelength for a 'reverse image' of the Third World."

These are the issues our partners should deal with. To my mind the Kairos Document has operated at this new level of partnership that goes beyond the usual funding relationship. It has not only had an impact here at home but it has also shaken the foundations of our partners. Although the *kairos* theologians were addressing the problems that concerned them here at home, the "reverse image" has had a tremendous impact in Europe and elsewhere. This has generated discussions on new forms of solidarity, what we have called "preventative solidarity" rather than "therapeutic solidarity."

The *Christian Aid News* editorial goes on to say that their "generosity" should attend to giving themselves time to hear the voices of those who can help them to find the answers. It says, "We need to listen to them . . . they will soon help us to open our eyes." This has to do with a reversed missionary role. Let me put it in the words of a participant at a Kairos Document meeting in London. He said that my presence there had a mission dimension. He said: "We need your missionaries; we are pagans, worshiping idols of traditions we have developed over the years; we are major contributors to the chaos in the world." Whereas people used to go to Europe to learn, he concluded the opposite must now happen.

We must therefore prepare ourselves to learn from one another, to exchange material, skills and resources; to share our experiences so that our faith can be enriched. This is where ecumenical theological interaction is necessary across the world. Just as we believe that there is no such thing as a "universal" theology with absolutes that apply to all situations and at all times, so we also believe that a contextual theological exercise which operates within a laager without exposure to or dialogue with the ecumenical family cannot be critical theology. We need to be in dialogue all the time as a universal Church of Christ.

As I have said before, the Kairos Document has started this new relationship of partnership which is now bearing fruit. Throughout the seven countries I visited, the Kairos Document was the major subject of discussion. The Kairos Document has made the church in Europe reflect on its own life and ask whether it is not just a replica of the church in South Africa that is being criticized in the

Kairos Document. A process of self-examination and critique is taking root both at an official church level and at a grass-roots level. The Kairos Document elicited responses and comments that have been very useful and enriching for those who are involved with the Kairos Document movement and engaged in the struggle for a just society in South Africa. But I want to suggest that this process be taken further. Instead of just responding to this theological reflection on the South African situation, I propose that churches in Europe and elsewhere now produce their own Kairos Documents. This can be done, as it was done in South Africa, by reflecting on your situation, criticizing your sociopolitical structures and your economic base, and by identifying the injustices in these structures and confronting them to remove the evil in them. This should be your mission to your people to save them from their sin and from the judgment that will follow.

The second dimension of your mission would be to criticize your church structures, traditions and practices which may be (and usually are) supporting and legitimizing this whole international crime of sin and death. How is your church party to the evils of this world? How far does the church collaborate in this evil? Remember always that the prophets of olden days always criticized the society around them and the priests who collaborated with it.

There are two levels or more at which this could be done. The first is at a level of the official church and its related ecumenical structures. The second level is at the grass roots, consisting of committed Christians in each country (and maybe collectively throughout Europe), in small and big groups. At both levels the activity should not only consist of reflection and criticism but of action to change the systems concerned. We must be engaged in an action-reflection-action process to be able to produce results. Your Kairos Document must be a by-product of your praxis, of your struggles for justice in your situation.

You should have realized that this whole exercise is inviting you to do contextual theology with us and share it with us at an ecumenical level. It is a call to struggle together to understand what God's will is for us in this chaotic world of pain and suffering.

Enough about this whole theory of a new form of solidarity and partnership. We are now on our way back home. It is interesting how tension builds up when one begins to fly home into that miserable, cruel and brutal apartheid system that kills like a machine or like the devil. We left Heathrow Airport and flew toward the west first, then southwest, and now we are heading southward.

Initially we were puzzled about why we flew to the west rather than south or in a southeasterly direction to South Africa, and why we did not go via Kenya, which would have been more logical. Consulting the map in the airline magazine reminded us that apartheid is such a crime against humanity and such a leper in the eyes of the world that it cannot be allowed to fly over Africa or touch down in Nairobi. One wonders what kind of a country allows South Africa to have a stopover. In the light of the resolution of the National Consultative Conference on the Crisis in Black Education that landing rights be denied to South Africa, Zimbabwe, Zambia and Malawi may have to review their position in this regard.

I want to take this opportunity of thanking every one of you, especially those who made my learning experience possible in such a short space of time. Thank you for your time, energy, efforts and resources. I hope that my visit will inspire a new perception of our mission in the world as a Church of Christ.

May God bless you all,

Sincerely yours,
Frank Chikane (Rev)

Letter to Friends
after the State of Emergency:
June 1986

June 26, 1986

Dear Friends,

Events have been happening so fast here that it seems like ages since I visited Europe. Maybe it is because since the last three weeks or so, the whole face of South Africa has changed radically. Suddenly people can be detained and kept in prison indefinitely or for periods of six months for no particular crime or misdeed. If a policeman thinks you should be removed, he can do so without explaining his action.

No publication of names of those who are detained is allowed. Even passing information from one family member to another about a detained brother or sister could constitute an offense. And in all this, one has no recourse to a court of law or justice. Because of this strange new face of South Africa, many people have disappeared and it is very difficult now to make out whether some are in detention, in hiding, dead or have left the country. Those who have some information, those who have seen residents in the township gunned down along the streets, cannot make their witness known.

This brings us to the WITNESS OF THE CHURCH IN SOUTH AFRICA. Is it still possible under circumstances where no one is allowed by "law" to criticize the regime, its State of Emergency, and its security forces? Is it still possible to be a conscience of the state? Is it still possible to minister effectively to the black masses of South Africa who are victims of this system when one cannot

85

talk about their suffering, pain and death? When one cannot even talk about the evil that is responsible for this death? The Catholic Church cannot even announce that its general secretary is detained or deported. The Evangelical Presbyterian Church cannot even announce that its moderator is detained. How does the Church carry out its mission under the circumstances?

Given this setup, the people of South Africa, especially the victims, are looking to the Church as their only salvation at this stage. It is possible that the Church could go on according to the emergency regulations where using a descriptive word (adjective) would fall within the law. Or is the Church going to submit and be quiet? Is this not the time when the whole Church should go to prison and join the people there rather than imprison itself by subjecting itself to those regulations? Is this not the time when the Church should say now in a louder voice than ever before that ''WE MUST OBEY GOD RATHER THAN MEN'' (Acts 5:29), when the Church is faced with the KAIROS in the country and in its history? Shouldn't the Church review what the Lordship of Christ means at this stage? This is the time, the moment of truth. As the Kairos Document says, there is ''no place to hide and no way of pretending to be what we are not in fact. At this moment in South Africa the Church is about to be shown up for what it really is and no cover-up will be possible'' (p.1).

Most of you will remember that I said after the end of March that if the Botha regime did not accede to the demands of the people there would only be two options in the offing for us: either the international community (particularly the USA, the UK, West Germany, France, Switzerland and Japan) put pressure on South Africa to change peacefully by talking to the people's leadership, or the other option is too ghastly to contemplate: a direct violent confrontation between the forces of apartheid and the oppressed masses of South Africa. This will be brutal, merciless and cost millions of lives, leaving a trail of maimed people and a devastated country. A determination of the people to die for their freedom and the determination of the regime to preserve white domination and apartheid at all costs spell only death and death ahead.

The tragedy of our situation is that these five western countries I referred to above and Japan have come out clearly that they are not going to apply pressure on their partners in the oppression and exploitation of the black people of South Africa. The fact is that unless these western powers and Japan are pressured by their own people, who must also be prepared to sacrifice in this regard, they are not going to move on a purely moral basis. Where capital, profits and powers are involved, there is no room for morality!

This leaves us with the option I said is too ghastly to contemplate. This option has already been embarked on, and the world is going to see the type of violence it has never seen before in the days ahead of us. Maybe we as South Africans are called to face this reality. May God help us to die in faith with a clear goal in mind, the kingdom of our Lord Jesus Christ.

Belonging to the one Body of Christ, we are looking forward to your solidarity, support and prayers in this regard.

Your fellow brother in Christ.

Frank Chikane (Rev.)
General Secretary

A Reflection on Our Life

by Kagiso Chikane

It is difficult for me to say when I met Frank Chikane for the first time. I met him several times in the Student Christian Movement's conferences where he was invited as a guest speaker. My first close contact with him was in 1973 when a Christian Youth Club called Teen Challenge Christian Club was opened in Naledi Township in Soweto. I was in a high school then, and he used to visit the club during the university holidays. I used to like him and enjoyed his company—a rare opportunity. Most of us used to view him as a big brother who was concerned with solutions to our problems.

To tell the truth, I was impressed by his preaching. Although he would use different biblical texts he seemed always to talk about the fact that "Jesus had compassion over the people and that somehow we have to imitate him." In one conference I remember him saying: "I refuse to be frustrated because Jesus in me was never, is never and will never be frustrated." I remember that together with my friends we used to quote this when we talked about him. To most of us he was a likeable person but also a difficult character to deal with. Difficult in the sense that he is not an extrovert and used to like to talk business. It was not easy to relax with him and have small talk with him. Not that he distanced himself from the people, but there was always a scramble to talk with him.

There was a day in 1974 when he made a great impression on me. Our school, Morris Isaacson High School, had undertaken a trip to the University of the North and we met Frank and some friends from Teen Challenge Christian Club there. We then went to a nearby village to see my neighbor's relatives. There were about five of us, and on our way to the village I found myself walking with Frank and I really felt some warmth in me about him. I asked him about that trip to the village and he also said he was quite impressed about it. Nothing came out of that trip, but I think it laid a good foundation for our love affair.

Although he had left the University of the North by the time I went there in 1975, we used to write friendly letters to each other. He used to take a long time before replying and I remember that together with Pinky (a friend of mine) we wrote him a letter accusing him of not replying to our letters. During the holidays he told us that he could not cope with correspondence owing to the fact that many people wrote to him. Between 1975 and 1977 our relationship was just cordial. I used to visit his home because I used to visit his father's congregation in Tladi. I had visited them on several occasions during his detentions. I had also visited him in Kagiso after his detention.

Our courtship started in 1978 when I was just about to complete my teacher's diploma. Although I knew I loved him, accepting his love proposal was not easy. I had to ask myself as to whether I would cope with the kind of life that I was going to live. The future did not look bright, especially with the detentions he had gone through. The possibilities of him being detained were not slim. In short, when I accepted it I knew that it meant taking him as he is and not trying to change him. My friends used to tease me by saying if I got married to Frank I'd be a breadwinner, and truly speaking I have been during his detentions.

During our courtship days I knew I was not going to have an easy life. I knew I was going to share him with others. This happened many a time, for he would break our appointments so as to be where he was "most needed." At times I would be mad about it and he would explain why he could not come and, well, I ended up accepting his apology.

Although I have never been actively involved in political activities, I learned a lot from Frank. My stay at the University of the North for four years was also an eye-opener to the sociopolitical and economic realities of our lives as blacks. Many times we found ourselves packing our bags and going home because of the boycotts and closure of the university. Many a time we ran away from the police during the boycotts and landed up in nearby villages and townships where we asked for accommodation because the campus was now under the "protection" of the police.

Frank never promised me any bright future except for his belief that God will take care of us and never forsake us. The closer I came to him, the more I learned to understand his reasons for being involved in church work and in the sociopolitical lives of the people. His involvement in the day-to-day lives of the people stemmed from his belief in a just and compassionate God who wanted everybody to have life more abundantly. This kind of God was the one who cared, who healed, who saved people from their sins, who hated oppression, who wanted justice to be meted out to all equally, irrespective of their race, color or creed: a God who has created enough food and all the resources for everybody. He thus believed in a God who would not let others starve when his earth could produce so much for all. This God could clothe the naked, could provide employment for the unemployed. He could liberate the prisoners because he had said in his Word: ". . . all should cast all their burdens on to him because he cares."

I then learned to understand that this God cannot descend from heaven to do all these things, but man had to be his instrument. Frank always seemed to be puzzled by people who tried to say, if you pray, God will provide. Even in his preaching he would grapple with what he used to call the vertical and the horizontal ministry. He would say there are Christians who say don't worry about earthly things because we are looking forward to a better world after death. This was the vertical ministry. The horizontal one refers to where people are involved in the sociopolitical, economic aspects of life and do not emphasize that people ought also to relate to God. He thus tried in his ministry to merge the two. Trying to merge the two landed him in trouble, especially with the former group. He was branded a non-Christian, a Communist, a politician, a pretender because he called himself a Christian while involving himself in "unchristian" activities.

Although I had thought that I knew him well and the kind of work he was doing when we got married in 1980, I later discovered when staying together that I did not. There was almost no privacy in that Kagiso mission house of the Apostolic Faith Mission Church. Actually it was the "people's house." Even the groceries we bought with our meager salaries were not ours alone. At times when I came back from work at a local high school, I would find that somebody had been busy cooking in the kitchen. This was really too much for me. Mad as I would be, because at times the food cooked would be what I intended to cook for supper, he would help me to come back to my senses by making me realize that one cannot leave a hungry man "to go in peace" without giving him his basic need, namely food. You cannot just say to him, "Well, brother or sister, I've heard about your problems. May the good God bless you."

Although he used to reassure me of his love, at times I felt like screaming at him to put more sense into him, just to have a break from his full program. We hardly had a free hour together without any interference. I remember saying to him one day, "Dear, I think I have to make an appointment with you because I hardly see you. Please make room for me in your diary."

Many a time I was faced by a very depressed husband. Depressed because he felt he had reached a stage where he could not help everybody who came to him. There would be a parent, wife, brother, sister or husband whose beloved member of the family had been detained, or a family where everybody was unemployed and thus could not pay rent or take children to school or buy necessities of life. At times it was a family without shelter, spouses with marital problems, young and old people looking for spiritual guidance—I can go on and on. Through the Kagiso Self-Help Scheme, established largely through Frank's efforts, most of the people got help. It was a legal center, a working center, a spiritual center. It was almost everything to the Kagiso community.

As I came closer to the lives of the community around us, my attitude changed. The question was, what was he to do when everybody came to him for help? Was he to tell them that he was still having supper or lunch or breakfast with his wife? Was he supposed to tell them that he could not help them so as not to go to jail? As my view of things changed, I realized that he did this out of pure compassion. It was not for self-esteem or any financial reward. It was because he was trying to merge the horizontal and the vertical ministry. I realized that his happiness was mine and mine was his. I learned that his happiness lay in him feeling he had achieved what he wanted to do. And now that I no longer saw his work as a burden but as part of his ministry of serving the God I also believed in, it became a real joy for me to know that our lives were a blessing to others. I learned to rejoice with him when solutions were found and support him when things were uphill.

When he was detained in 1980 during the whites' celebration of "The Freedom of Krugersdorp" it was as if life had come to a standstill for me. Other people were also detained, so as to make the celebration "a peaceful one," I suppose. By the afternoon the house was full of concerned relatives of the detained people and one could see frustration written in their faces when to their dismay the very person who was supposed to give them advice was also detained. He was detained during the day, while I was still at work. I did not know what to do. It was funny that suddenly I had to go through the agony of what other people had been going through. The question was, how long was he going to be detained? What was I going to do if he was not released soon? I just felt paralyzed. Some people consoled us by saying that they thought after the celebration most would be released, and this was true. We were so excited when he was released after the celebration. This was just the beginning of a series of hardships for us.

The year 1981 was tough for us. It was a year when our church decided to suspend him for "being involved in politics." At first it was unbelievable when he was called before the church council. It was unbelievable that people who call themselves Christians could formulate so many incoherent stories about a person. It also came as a shock when I discovered that Christian ministers can treat another minister in a way they treated Frank. I tried to be objective when looking at the events that led to his suspension. I asked myself how appearing in meetings where one is invited can cause such an uproar, whether it was a sin to help the needy. The accusations could not be substantiated but it was clear that no reasoning could change their minds about suspending him. It became worse when one of them indicated that he had met with the police and that they had given him information about Frank. We then knew that this was not simply a church matter.

On the other hand, in my analysis of the problem I realized that self-interest was also behind most of the pastors who were behind his suspension. In fact Frank was a threat to them. This is still the case because even now they cannot leave him alone. They were faced with a young man who was winning the hearts and minds of the young and the old. He was always constitutionally elected into most of the church portfolios, and from the local council to the national council of young people. Their positions were thus threatened. They could not pin him down on biblical grounds or constitutionally. They could not say as a church council: "This man is found guilty of committing the following sins." They knew that the language best understood by our missionaries would be: "He is involved in politics." It is really ironic that your fellow oppressed brothers, who can hardly have fellowship in the so-called white Church, say it is politics when you question this division of the Church into white, black, colored and Indian, or when you say there should be equality before the law.

In actual fact, while I was almost bitter about the whole situation, I came to understand their positions, which are like that of most of us blacks. It is a position of dependency on the white missionaries. Having a position in the church committee was a real achievement to them. They will always remind you that they are talking to you as chairmen, secretaries of the church, and so forth. This I heard many a time when they talked to me. The other problem is "lack of knowledge," as part of a deprived community which is to a large extent denied the right to education, and thus becomes open to manipulation. Because of this reality it was difficult to enter into any logical discussion with them.

We really agonized about the matter and when, finally, he was told of the year's suspension, it was a blow to the family. This condition would be reviewed if he repented from this sin of his commitment to the lives of the people, namely "involvement in politics."

I remember him coming home very depressed. He really had bad news for the family. It was shattering in the sense that his ministry, which we so cherished, which was part and parcel of our lives, could be brought so easily to an end by our fellow Christians. If they were saying he had misappropriated funds, committed a biblical sin or ignored the constitution, it would have been understood. The worst part of the story was that within two months we were supposed to have left the mission house. It meant leaving our beloved congregation, the youth club (the Interdenominational Youth Club), and the Self-Help Scheme, which had been such a blessing to the community. Actually I have to say, up till this day both of us still miss the life with a congregation. In spite of what Frank does now, he always talks about that congregation which had also learned to devote its life not only to God but to others. The decision meant that we had to look for alternative accommodation, and where were we supposed to start?

One thing he was clear about was that we would not leave the church. Actually people approached him to form a new and relevant church. His answer was that "God had enough problems with the existing churches and he did not want to add another problem." In the end we decided to remain in the church and be full members of his father's church. In spite of the fact that his credentials and ordination certificate were taken back by the church, we have regarded ourselves as full members of this very church which does not want him.

As if our problems were not enough, he was detained in November 1981, during the early hours of the 20th. It was at about 2:30 A.M. when we heard loud knocks on the doors and windows and torches were flashed on the windows. A male voice shouted, "Frank, open! The police!" I was frightened, shivering, and Frank remained calm. He was told to pack toiletries and he then took a few clothes. They never said anything to me and left with him. I could not sleep. I had lots of questions with no answers. I was numb. It was as if I had been told somebody I loved was dead. I was left alone with my eleven-month-old baby, Obakeng. I was not even given a letter to show that the people taking him were really policemen.

In the morning I informed my in-laws and lawyers about the matter. What would they do? Nothing. For the lawyers it was going to be confirmation of the fact and under what section he had been detained.

For people whose family members have never been detained, it is difficult to understand the emotions that some of us go through. They do not even understand why there are groups calling for the release of detainees. Together with Frank's friend we went from one police station to the other, and we were told he was not there. When we came back I was emotionally exhausted. I was not informed of his whereabouts by the police nor was I allowed to see him. It was a painful experience.

It was only after the death of Neil Aggett in detention that I was given permission to see Frank at John Vorster Square. Visiting him in prison was one of those joyous and painful moments in my life. I would look forward to the visit. I would be excited when I saw him, although it was always in the presence of a policeman who was there to listen to our conversation. I would then be engulfed by a great depression when we parted. At times it would go on for days. This would then put me under great stress. I would then recover and be grateful that he was still alive and okay. During the first months of his detention it was difficult for me to eat. I would say to myself, *Here am I eating while he may not be eating.* This pain was made worse by the pastors of our district council who came to me and told me I had to leave the church manse. I remember them telling me that Frank should have known and provided accommodation for us before involving himself in politics. They also wrote me letters telling me to leave the manse. What a terrible thing. They did not sympathize with me; they seemed to be rejoicing at my plight.

I went through a period of self-pity. Ultimately I got all the strength to stand. I can say God gave me the inner strength to face the world. My colleagues were sympathetic and even offered me some accommodation. I started to look at the problem differently. I thought of my loving husband, who would never harm or talk rudely or badly to anyone. He was a person who was ready to sacrifice for other people. I started to become very proud of him. He had not killed nor harmed anybody; his greatest sin or crime was to say God has created us equally and that he hates oppression. There was thus no need for me to be ashamed or to feel pity for myself. Actually, I told myself I had to stand up and be proud of him. If ever he was going to be released, he ought to find me patiently waiting for him. I told myself that as he always said, "I will never be frustrated because of the Jesus in me," I was not going to be frustrated, either.

Members of our congregation and the community were supportive. They used to be with me. They used to accompany me to the police station to take food and clothing to him, but they were not allowed to see him. When the district pastors wanted me to leave the church and to bring another minister, the congregation opposed them. They said to them: "If our pastor has sinned, show us the woman with whom he was involved in adultery." They asked them the meaning of "involvement in politics." They really protected me. They said they would never accept another pastor except Frank. In the meantime pressure through letters was put on me by our district pastors to leave the manse.

Because our God is a good shepherd he helped me through difficulties to get the house in Soweto. I wish to say getting it was a real miracle. In the first place the building contractors and the building society did not want to allow me to have a bond because my husband was detained and, according to them, what guarantee did I have that he would be released? If he was not released, how would I pay for the bond? While my church, which belonged to the Pentecostal Churches or "spiritual Churches," was throwing me out, other churches hearing of my plight were opening their doors to me. Through one of Frank's friends, one of the churches helped me get the house. Before his detention, Frank had just been promised a temporary job by the Institute for Contextual Theology (ICT). I went to the institute and they gave me all the backing. They wrote an affidavit which I sent to the building society to the effect that they would pay for the bond. This really made me say, "The Lord is my shepherd, I shall not want." I pleaded for an extension of time from my district committee pastors but I was told that by the end of April I must move out of the manse. Getting a house was part of God's blessings to make his children eat before their enemies, because I got the keys for the house on the last day of April and moved into the new house on May 1, 1982.

A week before our departure, our congregation decided to bid me farewell. To our amazement one pastor from our local district committee came and put a big lock at our Kagiso church so that no function could be held there. Emotions ran high in the congregation but we decided to hold my farewell function outside the church instead of breaking in. My bitterness toward them had waned. I came to understand them and really to say they did not know what they were doing. I realized that my Christian life should not be destroyed by what people did to me. Mine was just to trust in God. Our parting with the congregation was a painful one.

I went to a new area in Soweto and stayed with my brother, my sister-in-law and Obakeng. During this time I was allowed to visit my husband in prison. He was excited to see me and I used to look forward to seeing him. At times we felt that if he was charged it would be better because he would be sentenced and we would then know about his future. It is really frustrating when you do not know about your fate. On the other hand, the other question always on my mind was why I wished that he should be charged when he had not committed any crime. Well, in times like these you have to battle through these contradictions and still live above your problems. Detention without trial is really bad. It separates kids from their parents, wives from their husbands and vice versa. Frank's parents wanted to see him but were not allowed to. This separation was painful for them, too. Every time I went to see Frank they would pass their regards. They had to accept the fact that they would not be allowed to see their son. All of us had to wait prayerfully for his return.

His release in July 1982 was such a joyous moment for us. His parents phoned me at work and told me he was there. I could not believe it. I rushed there and I was very excited. I had to take him with all the pride in me to his own home which he had never seen before. One other interesting thing that I did not mention was the fact that I had obtained a driver's license during his detention. In his absence I was always frustrated when I had to do things like going to see the lawyers in Johannesburg, and even doing some family errands. It meant asking people to drive me and this dependence frustrated me. He was amazed that I could drive so well when I took him home.

One thing I learned during this detention was that, as a woman, I have to learn to be independent. I should not depend on anyone because everybody has his or her own problems. I had to ask for help when it was absolutely necessary. Driving thus made life a little bit easier for me. I no longer put Obakeng on my back on my way to work during rainy days and moaned about Frank's detention. I learned to do many things, and when I could not do them, I taught myself never to say, "If Frank was around he could have done them." The Bible became real to me. I learned to say I can do all things through Christ who gives me strength. Frank was very proud of me and showed his appreciation.

He went to the ICT and another hectic program started. In 1983, when the United Democratic Front (UDF) was launched, he was hardly home. In February 1985 the same experience of November 1981 repeated itself. Policemen came at about 3:00 in the morning with a warrant of arrest. He was told he was arrested for high treason. We looked at each other. Then I packed lots of clothing for him and off they went with him. I thought if it is high treason it means seeing him for the last time. Somehow we were expecting his detention, but not for high treason. Some of his UDF friends had been detained, and we knew he would be detained. Lots of preparations were made about the house, his work, etc. But detention is detention; you cannot simply get used to it.

When he was detained in 1981, Obakeng was still young and did not understand, but now he was the one who asked lots of questions. He thought his father was a criminal because the policemen always arrested criminals on TV. I had to tell him Frank was not one but was detained because the police did not like what he was saying. I had gone with him to the Jabulani Amphitheatre when the community was rejoicing with Archbishop Tutu after he was awarded the peace prize. Frank was also there on stage. I had to say to Obakeng that the police really disliked what he said on that day. This answer seemed to satisfy him. I did not know that my simple reply meant so much to him, till one day after Archbishop Tutu had visited our home. It was a real pastoral visit which was really meaningful to me. After his departure, my son said to me, "Mom, you said Daddy was arrested because he spoke at the amphitheatre?" I said yes. He said, "Why is the Archbishop not detained, because he also spoke there?" I was shocked by his analysis. I said to him, "I do not know." One thing that struck me about that question was that it meant he had accepted my explanation about his father's detention.

It is really difficult to expect a child to understand under such circumstances, but I made up my mind that I had to make him feel proud about Frank. I told him of all the things he did for the people which landed him in jail. He seemed to appreciate what he did. When I went with him to Durban during the trial we stayed at Paul David's house. I told him that he was not the only one whose father was detained because Paul was also in the treason trial. When we met Mandela, Aubrey Mokoena's son who is almost the same age as Obakeng, I told him that Mandela's father was also detained.

This meeting with other children of the detained people seemed to be meaningful to him. His exposure to them made him remember that his father was not the only one who was detained, and that other children were also having to do without their fathers.

The thought of never seeing Frank for perhaps twenty years if he was sentenced brought lots of depression to me. It is really difficult to cope with your emotions and those of kids aged five and six months. Although Otlile, our second son, was a quiet baby, when he cried he used to bring me to tears—especially when he was sick. There were moments when I asked myself how was I going to cope. There is a thought which revived my spirit always: I looked around me and saw that there were many women, widows, divorced and other single parents who never got married, who had children to look after. Most of them had no alternative but to be single mothers. Life was going on for them. I vowed that life should also continue for me. In my mind I said to myself, *These women are separated from their beloved husbands or boyfriends and may never be reunited to them. On that score, who am I not to accept my situation?* Our separation was different from that of these women. We still loved each other, but his noble convictions led to our separation. Honestly speaking, this thought kept my mind from sinking to despair. I told myself that I had kids to take care of and they had nobody except myself. So, if I became a nervous wreck or tried to console myself with liquor so as to remove frustrations, what would become of them? In spite of my problems, I had my own life to live. I also was entitled to a happy life no matter what happened to my husband. I decided to try to protect my kids and to try to give them what they would have if Frank was present. I straightened my back again and, with the help of God, the wives of the other detainees, and friends I managed to cope.

We used to meet regularly with the other Treason Trialists' wives and this made our morale high. All of us were very proud of our husbands. Instead of discouraging one another, we used to encourage ourselves. Their release in May 1985 came as a shock to me. I heard about it over the radio. I couldn't believe it. I started phoning around some of the Treason Trialists' families, and this was confirmed. Oh, that joy that was in me!

When I met him at the airport I could not believe it. The kids were overwhelmed with joy. During the night I remember waking up and pinching him. I wanted to make sure I was not dreaming. The bail was granted on a Friday.

Our joy was shortlived because on Monday, early in the morning, we woke up with our bedroom and sitting room on fire. Gasoline bombs were thrown at our house. My baby was sleeping next to the window and the curtains were on fire. Confusion reigned. Frank took the baby, Otlile, out of the room and we started to extinguish the fire. Neighbors heard our screams and rushed to our house. It was a sad and frightening experience for us. We were grateful that none of us had sustained any serious injuries. Psychologically a lot of harm was done. I could no longer sleep peacefully without worrying about bombs. Waking up in the middle of the night to find your house on fire is not a nice experience. We have slowly gone through it, although, with so many enemies, you always expect the worst.

While we were trying to recover from this experience, somebody told Frank that he was a member of an assassination squad and that Frank and others were on a hit list. Frank and some prominent people of our community were supposed to be murdered. This was more than a blow. For the first time in our lives, we realized that we were walking in the valley of the shadow of death. This was a worse experience. This man had really endangered his life by telling Frank and his friends who were also on the hit list. It reminded us of the prophet Elijah who revealed the secret of the enemies to the king of Israel. We were grateful to this man. The matter was left in the hands of the police. After some investigation by Frank's lawyers, nothing came out of this case till today. This matter really showed us that we live by God's grace. Some of us really mean it when we pray in the night, saying, "Father, your word says you never sleep nor slumber, please watch over us tonight." In the morning when we say, "Lord, thank you for your protection," we really mean it.

When charges were dropped against the Treason Trialists in December 1985, we were excited. Their acquittal came as a real surprise. Frank was a criminal in the eyes of the state and suddenly he was free. What a relief for the family, especially because we had lived under stringent bail conditions. His bail conditions were to report daily to the local police station in the morning and afternoon. He was supposed to be indoors by 9:00 P.M. I used to be worried when he did not come home before nine. I would always ask him whether he had reported to the police station. I would wait for him if I thought he was late and he would then enter the yard quickly and I would park the car in the garage so as not to be found after nine outside the yard.

After the Treason Trial we were so relieved. We thought a new book of life was going to be opened where we would live a relatively "normal" life (because I regard this as an abnormal one). We thought we would never experience any other problem compared to the Treason Trial. We were cheating ourselves. The state of emergency was declared in June 1986 and we had to live like two silly teenagers, madly in love with each other, but hiding from parents who would kick all the dust if they found them together. I will close our chapter of life here; I cannot say much about life under the state of emergency because we are still living under it.

I have talked more about our public life and I believe most people will be interested in knowing our personal life. Believe me or not, I have not seen what Frank has written in the chapters of this book because we felt I would be influenced by what he has written. Even now, as I am concluding this chapter, I do not know the contents of the other chapters. He asked me to write whatever I wanted to write about our life experiences.

I believe most of the people who know Frank will tell you that he is not an emotional person. He is a meticulous person. That is how he is at home. I still wish to hear somebody who will tell me that he saw him very angry and shouting at others. For the seven years we have stayed together, I have not seen him in that mood. He is such a loving husband and I am glad to say during all these hard times I never forget all the warmth I got from him. In his absence during detentions, or when he was in hiding during the state of emergency, deep in my heart I would say to myself there are men around me but my husband remains the best of them all. Although he never spends a lot of time with our kids, he is a darling to them. At times I feel jealous when they tend to confide more in him than in me. When they make mistakes he calls them and talks to them. I always admire him because it seems as if I always shout at them when they become silly. His character has thus made me stand by him through thick and thin.

APPENDIX I

Statement by Frank Chikane from the 1985 Treason Trial

Frank Chikane, Accused Number 10, States

1. I was born on the 3rd of January 1951, at Orlando, Johannesburg. My father, a priest, is James Chikane, and my mother Erenia Chikane. I have six brothers and sisters—Rodpers (37), Abraham (28), Thabile (22), Dorcas (20), Salome (18) and Khotso (16).

Academic Training

2. My primary education was undertaken at Hlolohelo Primary School (1960–1962), and Tau-Pedi Higher Primary School (1963–1966), both in Soweto. I began my secondary schooling at Naledi Secondary School (1967–1969), and completed my matriculation at Orlando High School (1970–1971).

3. In 1972 I enrolled at the University of the North (Turfloop), Pietersburg. I registered for a BSc degree.

My studies were disrupted during my third year of study (1974), mainly as a result of the "Viva FRELIMO" rallies which celebrated the independence of Mozambique. These rallies led to the arrest of many students and long sit-ins and boycotts of university classes. I was not arrested as a result of these rallies, but they affected my involvement in student affairs, as indicated below.

4. I could not return to University the following year (1975) and I taught at Naledi High School for a few months.

The arrest of students at Turfloop led to a six-day sit-in. After

103

this sit-in, there were only eight days before the October 1974 examinations. As a trustee of the Student Aid Fund, I was exceptionally pressured (organizing defense, finance, contact with the families of the detained, and providing leadership to the student body during this crisis period). As a result, the added pressure of examinations led to my having a breakdown during an examination session. I was taken to hospital by university authorities. As a result I missed two of my final papers. Despite my illness, the university refused permission for me to write aegrotat examinations.

My bursary was therefore withdrawn for 1975. The student body was prepared to raise money for me to continue studying, but I was told by a sympathetic member of staff that I would be victimized if I came back to the university, and that the state might also harass me.

After this, I joined a crusade of my church (the Apostolic Faith Mission). This crusade, called "Christ For All Nations," made me part of an evangelical mission which I felt was my calling. I saw my participation in the struggles of students at the University as part of my Christian responsibility to contribute to the making of justice and peace, and to alleviate the pain and suffering of students I ministered to. I had a commitment to the Lord even before I went to the University, and knew that I was called to be his servant on earth.

Student involvement helped to reinforce my commitment, and enabled me to develop a better theological understanding from experience of oppression, suppression and exploitation.

Because I had an evangelical background, it was natural that I joined the Christ for All Nations Crusade. There were a lot of theological contradictions which confronted me during this period, and thus forced me to review the whole system of Christian theology.

I became convinced, over the course of time, that the tradition of theology in our churches was a western theology—a theology from the context of the oppressors, an imperialist theology of domination.

Theological Training

5. During 1975 I registered with the Pan-African Bible College, a correspondence division of our Bible College. I registered to undergo

theological training so as to qualify as a minister.

6. Once I had completed half the course, I was engaged as an evangelist for the church. In June 1976 I was placed in a congregation (Assembly) in Kagiso Township, Krugersdorp, as a practicing pastor under supervision.

7. After completing the course, thereby obtaining a Diploma in Theology in 1979, I was placed on probation for one year. I was ordained as a Pastor in March 1980.

Challenge to My Faith

8. I grew up as a black child in the ghetto of Soweto, subjected to ghetto education. At the age of around 16, life became one of hide and seek, because of police harassment. They raided the townships for so-called pass offenders, and thus victimized children of our age in establishing whether we were of pass-carrying age or not.

My first experience of direct confrontation was with some young white policemen, who assaulted me because I addressed them as "meneer" instead of "baas." This was contrary to what I was taught at school, in terms of addressing people with respect.

I was challenged by our situation at school in relation to the apartheid system to defend my faith and my witness. Students, or for that matter other victims of apartheid, confronted me with the reality that those who created and maintain this system are or claim to be Christians; that those who dispossessed us at the point of a gun did so in the name of "Christ"; that those who exploit workers at the work place are called Christian, and some even make you pray.

If even those who preach the Gospel discriminate and perpetuate apartheid, the victims of that system were bound to ask critical questions about the Christian faith.

Faced with this situation, I had to separate apartheid from the Word of God. I had to critically expose the lie behind the then-acclaimed basis for apartheid. I had to restate the truth of God's Gospel which had been negated by the system of apartheid. I had to tender my witness to the world in defense of my faith.

9. This happened as early as my high school days. Students challenged members of the Student Christian Movement (SCM), which I had belonged to from secondary school days, to justify their faith. The challenging students took this faith to be an instrument of their

oppressors. They argued that western missionaries collaborated with the western colonialists by introducing the Christian faith to "soften" the aborigines of this land. This was to make them humble, to enable the invaders of this land to dispossess the people. A popular expression then was that "the white man exchanged the Bible for the land of the people."

10. Historical evidence was advanced to back up this analysis, especially the event where the Boers prayed before they waged war against the aborigines of this country, and declared that if God would help them win the war they would build a church for God. They fulfilled their "covenant" with their God—which students at the time called the "white god," and laid a gun on top of the Bible to signify this gross distortion of the grace and covenant of God.

This is a reality that confronts us as Christians—that our faith has been misused and misrepresented. The challenge is to differentiate between the faith itself, and those who misuse it for their own benefit. Some do so consciously, others unconsciously. It was important for me to critique these horrifying historical events which negated the Gospel, and to advance a liberating understanding of it. This would be the only way to approximate the kingdom of God on earth, a kingdom characterized by love, justice and peace.

The SCM (and hence my involvement in it) must be understood as a social institution, like any other (including the Church). It is therefore subject to social forces in society. As such, the SCM had also to be cleansed and liberated from the bondage of evil ideologies and systems.

11. More shattering evidence has been brought to light showing how missionaries collaborated with the system. I can if necessary elaborate on this historically, using the writings of Cecil John Rhodes, and Dr J.V. de Vries.

12. When I arrived at the University of the North in 1972, I found that the SCM was "banned" from campus by students. They felt that it made black people subservient and good "Bantus," not questioning any wrong practiced against them. It made them worry about heavenly things while the system oppressed and exploited them.

Because of this "banning," Christians prayed on top of the mountain next to the University.

13. Challenged by this situation, I participated in a mission of

reinterpretation and re-reading of the Bible. We faced the issues of the day with the Gospel of the Lord helping students to discover the power and the truth of the Gospel. I began to realize that the Christian faith was revolutionary, with the potential for changing society dramatically.

Involvement in Student Politics

14. During 1973 and 1974, I was involved with the "Evangelistic Fellowship" at the University. This ministered to students on campus, and reached out to many schools and institutions within 100 km radius of the University. We also reached out to other black universities, and also to the SCM in Lesotho.

15. When I arrived at the University of the North (1972), I automatically became a member of the South African Students Organization. At that stage, membership was acquired by registration at the University.

But this membership was short-lived. SASO was suspended by the University Administration after the closure of the University following the expulsion of Ongopotse Abraham Tiro.

16. SASO continued to exist off campus, until it was reinstituted in August 1984, when I once more officially became a member.

17. In September 1974, students celebrated the freedom of Mozambique. This led to the arrest of a number of students and student leaders, while others were forced to leave the country. (This was dealt with in S vs Cooper and others—the SASO/BPC trial of 1975–6). This action was followed by a sit-in at the University, which lasted for six days.

18. During this crisis I was elected by the student body (with Griffiths Zabala and Ishmael Mkhabela) as trustees of a fund established for the defense of detained students. Besides assuming the responsibilities of the Students Representative Council (leadership of the student body), we were also commissioned to organize lawyers for the defense of charged students, and to keep contact with the families of those detained.

19. All the trustees were Christians who participated with me in Christian witness on campus, as referred to above. Our election was a show of trust and confidence in our Christian commitment to justice and peace.

20. In the subsequent inquiry into the unrest on campus, (the

Snyman Commission), I gave evidence on behalf of the student body. The Commission wrongly represented me as a SASO member who infiltrated the Student Christian Movement (SCM), which the Commission claimed was responsible for the unrest.

This is incorrect. I was chairperson of the SCM at Naledi Secondary School in 1969, before I had even heard of SASO, which was then in its formation.

21. It is sometimes suggested that I have, since my student days, changed my political position from a "black consciousness" one to a "charterist" position. I dispute this. At the time of my involvement with student politics, and to some extent SASO, there was no perceived conflict between black consciousness and political support for the Freedom Charter. Black consciousness aimed to deal with questions of consciousness, pride in being black, assertiveness, ending reliance on white leadership, etc. It was only much later that a conflict emerged between new-style black consciousness organizations, and the Freedom Charter position. I do not see any conflict between black consciousness and the Freedom Charter, except that different issues are addressed by these two positions. A conflict only arises when people begin to associate the Freedom Charter with the ANC. This conflict emerges, both because of their negative attitude to the ANC, and because of power politics, where people begin to look for differences to reinforce their personal interests. As I do not associate the Freedom Charter with the ANC exclusively, I do not see a conflict between support for it and black consciousness.

Further Theological Development

22. While working with Christ for All Nations as an administrative officer, I continued with this ministry until I started pastoral work in June 1976.

A few months before the June 1976 student uprisings, I conducted prayers at the Morris Isaacson High School, where Tsietsi Mashinini (first SRC president) was a student. The success of this devotional session led to students in the SCM organizing a major evangelistic service for the school. This was held at the Methodist Youth Centre, next to the school.

23. After proclaiming the Gospel in this session, I was criticized by Tsietsi Mashinini in the plenary session. He called me a victim

of white propaganda, obsessed by the white man's oppressive religion. Although I was called names, I explained my faith as a reinterpreted Gospel, liberated from western oppressive categories.

24. This whole experience and confrontation with the victims of apartheid forced me to reread the Bible with a critical eye, and to develop a liberation theology free from western Babylonic captivity.

25. The week I began my placement in Kagiso, Krugersdorp, as a pastor was followed by Wednesday, June 16, 1976. These events set the scene within which I had to minister—one of dissatisfaction, confrontation, frustration and violence.

Previous Detentions, Arrests, Charges, Involvement in Trials

26. I was detained under Section 6 of the Terrorism Act for seven days in January–February 1977, and held at John Vorster Square. I was subjected to torture by the security police, who believed I had a connection with the events which led to the charge of John Phala and others. I had no connection with them, and was released without charge. I do not recall making a written statement during this detention.

27. I was again detained under Section 6 from 6 June 1977 until January 1978. I was held in Krugersdorp, where I was subjected to long periods of torture. On my release I was charged (with public violence?) and granted bail of R200. Seven days after my release from detention, on the day I was due to appear in court, I was redetained at about 2:00 A.M., and terribly assaulted before I appeared in court at 2:00 P.M., rather than the scheduled 9:00 A.M. Charges against me were then withdrawn.

28. Subsequently, I testified for the defense in the Bethal PAC trial.

29. In 1980, I was detained for three days. This was just a day before P. W. Botha was to receive the freedom of Krugersdorp, which the community boycotted (except for community councillors). I was released a day after the Botha ceremony, having not been interrogated.

30. On 20 November 1981, I was detained by the Protea security police, who handed me over to John Vorster Square in January 1982. I was finally released without charge on 7 July 1982.

During this detention I was forced to make an untrue statement concerning my activities. I signed this statement, but refused to sign it under oath.

On my release, I was subpoenaed under Section 205 of the Criminal Procedure Act to answer certain questions. I answered these questions by denying knowledge of the meetings mentioned. My attorney in this matter was Priscilla Jana.

31. I testified for the defense in the SASO/BPC trial, S vs Cooper and others.

32. In addition, as previously mentioned, I testified before the Snyman Commission investigating unrest at the University of the North.

Relations with Ecumenical and Other Organizations

33. After my release from detention in January 1978, I participated, as an extension of my ministry, in the establishment of the Inter-denominational Youth Christian Club (IYCC). This club committed itself to what was called a two-dimensional ministry involving the spiritual and the social, the vertical and the horizontal. As evangelicals, we pledged to balance the "pendulum" by introducing the horizontal (social) dimension of our ministry.

In pursuance of this goal, we established a Social Welfare Department which initiated and facilitated Self-Help Projects in Kagiso. These consisted of child care, care for the aged, care for the blind, sewing, knitting, extra-tuition programs, adult education, and an information center.

The church was used as a center until a structure was erected on the premises where all the projects were housed and administered from.

34. I subsequently participated in the formation of the Krugersdorp Residents Organization (KRO), which addresses the problems, grievances and needs of that community.

35. I had been ordained in 1980, but was forced to stop ministering to my congregation in August 1981. I had been accused, on a number of times, by my church for my involvement in community projects and "politics." During August 1981 I was suspended by the West Rand District Council of my church. This suspension was upheld by the National Executive Council in October 1981. The suspension was to last for one year (until October 1982), when

I would be reinstated. I spent most of my suspension in detention (November 1981–July 1982). On my release, I requested a meeting with the top leadership of my church to clarify the issue that pertained to my suspension so that when October 1982 came, I could be reinstated without problems.

The letter from the West Rand District Committee suspending me read as follows:

"The Committee has suspended you from the 6th August, 1981, for the following reasons: that you are still active in politics, but that on the 31st January, 1980, you have promised the committee to be away from politics. The committee found that you are still appearing in the newspaper."

This letter was dated 7th August 1981.

In endorsing the suspension, the National Executive Council of the Church wrote:

"In view of the fact that Pastor Frank Chikane did not keep the promise he made regarding the conditions of his ordination, and because this Council finds that there is no change in his attitude, he be suspended from full-time ministry for 12 months from 28 October, 1981, in the hope that there will be a change of heart."

This was dated 30 October 1981.

The only evidence against me was press clippings where I was reported to be speaking/preaching at conferences and meetings. As I was not a member of any political party "outlawed" as "active," I requested clarification so that there would be no misunderstanding with the church in the future.

In my discussion with the president of the church, his general secretary and mission director, I was told that I would be reinstated if I was not involved in politics, I did not appear in the press, and I was not detained.

Although I was prepared to negotiate the first condition to some extent, I indicated that the other two were impossible, as they were not in my control. It was then suggested that I stop attending meetings and conferences where I could be reported in the press. I saw this blanket condition as an inroad into my ministry.

When October 1982 came, I was told that the matter was on the agenda. Since then, up to the present, I have not heard from the council except for a letter asking me to send back their credentials and the ordination certificate.

I did not contest this, as I thought it would be futile. By this time, I was already director of the Institute for Contextual Theology.

36. In September 1982 I was engaged as a full-time co-ordinator with the Institute of Contextual Theology (ICT). I was appointed general secretary of the ICT in 1983.

In these capacities, I participated in facilitating and initiating various projects which dealt with theology in the context of conflict in Southern Africa. These projects include programs on the theology and training of African independent churches, black theology of liberation, feminist theology, ministry in a conflict situation (MUCCOR), and various workshops, seminars and conferences reflecting on theological issues.

37. Because of this involvement, I have become a member of
- The Ecumenical Association of African Theologians in Southern Africa (EAATSA);
- The Ecumenical Association of African Theologians (EAAT); and
- The Ecumenical Association of Third World Theologians (EATWOT).

38. During my 1981–2 detention, my family was evicted from the church in Kagiso, and they settled in Soweto in my absence, while I was in detention. After my release, in 1982, I joined my family in Soweto, and became a member of the Soweto Civic Association (SCA) which was then led by the Committee of Ten. In 1984 I was elected deputy vice president of the SCA, which office I still hold.

39. In 1983 I participated in the discussions that led to the formation of the United Democratic Front (UDF). I was elected vice president of the UDF's Transvaal region, and I remained in that position until April 1985, when a new executive was elected.

The Freedom Charter

40. I had heard of, and seen copies of, the Freedom Charter in the first part of the 1970s. But I only read it carefully when it received considerable press coverage in the late 1970s and early 1980s. Attacks on the Freedom Charter, both from government spokesmen and some anti-apartheid organizations, also made me decide to study it so as to form my own opinion.

41. In my view, the Freedom Charter is the most unique grass-

roots document in South African politics. It evolved out of a two-year campaign aimed at getting as many people as possible to articulate their grievances and declare their vision for a just and peaceful South Africa. It was adopted at the Congress of the People in 1955, of which Professor Z.K. Mathews said:

"We want a gathering to which ordinary people will come, sent there by the people. Their task will be to draw up a blueprint for the free South Africa of the future."

42. The organizations involved in the Congress of the People were: the African National Congress, the South African Coloured People's Organization, the South African Congress of Trade Unions, the South African Indian Congress, and the Congress of Democrats. I believe that this gathering was the most representative political gathering in South African history. It therefore gives the Freedom Charter more legitimacy than any other document or constitution.

43. The state alleges that the "Revolutionary Alliance" regards the Freedom Charter as its political program and policy, and that therefore the Freedom Charter can only be implemented in South Africa through a violent revolution. I disagree. Whether the Revolutionary Alliance regards the Freedom Charter as its political program and policy or not, I regard the Charter as a people's document expressing the demands and vision of ordinary people in South Africa. I do not regard the Charter as the property of any one organization.

44. To suggest that the Charter can only be implemented through violent revolution is a direct negation of the very spirit of the Charter. The last part of the Charter, under the heading "There Shall Be Peace and Friendship," states that South Africa shall strive to maintain world peace and the settlement of all international disputes by negotiations, not war. While this refers to the international arena, I believe it embodies the spirit of the Charter in general.

45. I believe that the Charter is a most democratic document, setting out just ideals acceptable to most peace-loving nations. It is fully compatible with the UN Declaration of Human Rights. It allows "living space" and possibilities for those who have hitherto been oppressors. Thus, the Charter does not exclude the possibility of changing the view of the adversary, and allows for reconciliation. This is a basic tenet of the Christian faith.

46. The Freedom Charter also expresses strong Christian values. The respect for human dignity irrespective of color, race, sex or creed is important. It advocates equality for all humanity, and upholds the Christian ideal of sharing and freedom of association.

47. The use of the words "justice and peace" is a use of the characteristically descriptive words for the kingdom of God. As a servant of that kingdom, I am committed to these ideals as a Christian.

The South African Congress of Trade Unions (SACTU)

48. To me, SACTU is an historical reality that I heard of in historical records. I know that SACTU participated in the Congress of the People, and that due to repression it could not continue its work in the country, but was never banned. I know little more about SACTU.

The South African Communist Party (SACP)

49. I know even less about the SACP. I know it existed in South Africa, but was banned in 1950 and was accordingly not a party to the Congress of the People.

The African National Congress and the Armed Struggle

50. The history of the ANC, as I have referred to it in my speeches, went through over forty years of peaceful protest—making representations to those who held power, mass protest meetings, demonstrations, strikes and a defiance campaign. This tradition of peaceful protest was met by state violence to maintain apartheid.

51. The ANC also called, and I believe this call still stands, for a national convention to remove apartheid peacefully. These calls have been ignored.

52. As I understand it, the government's refusal to heed ANC calls, the use of repressive violence, together with the frustration of being ignored, silenced and punished, pushed the naturally peaceful ANC to resort to sabotage, violence and an armed struggle. The violence of the state gave birth to such violence as the ANC has undertaken.

53. But the ANC did not resort to an arbitrary choice of violence. In the view of its leaders, all peaceful methods had been

exhausted. It was only with the greatest reluctance that the ANC began a campaign of sabotage.

54. I believe that if South Africa could be declared an open society today, where all stood equal before the law, and where all had the right to participate in deciding the sort of society they want, the ANC would lay down its arms and participate in a peaceful process of change.

55. But the key to peace and nonviolent change is in the hands of those in power.

56. I do not believe that those in the ANC are intrinsically violent. I have known some of the young children who left the country after the 1976 upheavals and after, and who came back as ANC fighters. I taught some of them in Sunday school (e.g. my brother Abie Chikane, M. Ranato, David Matsone and others). I knew them as committed Christians, and some were leaders of young people in the church. They were out and out against violence, basing their understanding on the traditional theological position of the church. But somehow, because of the repressive nature of the state, because of the violence meted against them and the resulting theological contradictions, the discontinuities in their system of faith as young Christians—somehow they became members of the ANC and Umkhonto we Sizwe.

57. I cannot turn my back on these people, even if they have turned to violence. They were, and remain, my brothers and sisters. I cannot remain unaffected by the reasons why people I am called to minister to turn to violence. I cannot reject them because they have adopted a path that is not my own.

58. I am not an ANC member or active supporter. I have not chosen the path of violence or armed struggle. But I can understand those who have done so—and I cannot reject them for this.

My Attitude to Violence

59. My attitude to violence is based on my Christian faith. I am not a pacifist, who would refuse to participate in any form of violence (whether it be practiced by the state or those resisting it). But I do agree with those pacifists (the historical peace churches) who engage in nonviolent measures to try to influence the perpetrators of injustice. They try to convince the perpetrators of injustice that survival and the right to exist can be secured in striving for a joint

solution. They attempt to make the perpetrators of injustice aware of the consequences of their actions.

60. As much as I am against the violence of the state against blacks, I would be against any violence meted out by blacks against whites in a postapartheid society. I have persistently stated in public that if this happens, I will be back in the cells!

61. But I believe that a nonviolent strategy must be coercive as well as persuasive.

62. The "just war" theory was helpful in considering the question of war in the history of the Church. But it does not adequately address the problems of our day, and is accordingly not a solution to a Christian's attitude to violence. *Inter alia*, it does not address itself to the problem of an internal conflict with a dictatorship that is blatantly unjust.

63. It may be that there is a theological basis to extend the just war theory to "just revolution" and "justifiable resistance." But basically I am of the opinion that violence is undesirable and to be avoided as much as possible in resolving conflict. Although I am aware of the shortcomings of nonviolent methods in a country like South Africa, I have chosen to adopt this approach.

64. This decision was initially based on blind faith derived from the traditional theological position of the Church. This was really a theology of the *status quo* (a theology of counter-revolution). Here, the violence of the state is accepted without question. This is understandable because this attitude served the dominant classes in society, who controlled the Church.

65. But I was eventually faced with the contradiction of a blatantly unjust system, where the people I ministered to felt they had to defend themselves. I tried to develop a different theological basis for my position on violence.

66. I am challenged, because of my commitment to Christ, to exhaust all nonviolent methods of change to satisfy my conscience that I have tried everything possible before resorting to violence to affect change.

67. It is for this reason that I chose to participate in the formation of the IYCC (Interdenominational Youth Christian Club) with its related community projects; and KRO (Krugersdorp Residents Organization). These used peaceful methods to bring about change.

68. It is for this reason that I became part of the Soweto Civic

Association when I came to Soweto in 1982, and agreed to address meetings on the need for change.

69. And it is for this reason that I participated in the formation of the United Democratic Front, which was formed against the reservations of some who argued that there was no place for such a peaceful organization in South Africa at this stage.

70. I felt that even if there were difficulties in this approach, there was still room for a nonviolent strategy, in the sense that one was making oneself available to be violently acted against. From 1974 until the present, I believe that I have shown that all nonviolent means of resistance have brought forth violence against peaceful action: at the FRELIMO Rally (Turfloop, September 1974), in Soweto and elsewhere (1976 and after). I have myself been subjected to the violence of the apartheid system for being involved in nonviolent strategies of change. I have been detained five times since 1977, and during two of these detentions I was horribly tortured, assaulted, and held incommunicado for long periods.

71. I am prepared, if necessary, to go through whatever pain I have to for the sake of peace and justice, and for the gospel of reconciliation. This means that, despite its apparent lack of success, I remain committed to a nonviolent strategy of change, for the reasons set out above.

72. On the other hand, I have witnessed with understanding the growing violent resistance to South Africa's political system. This is a reality, based on history. From my own experience I can understand why some have resorted to such methods.

My Attitude to Revolution, and Its Meaning in My Speeches

73. The word "revolution" in my theological tradition is commonly used. It came into the language of theology as early as the 1960s, in the form of "the theology of revolution." Professor David Bosch observes this development in his book, *Witness to the World* (1980), pp. 213–14. He states that in the 1920s the Church accepted that there was a need for societal structures to be altered to bring about justice. But this change had to be gradual and evolutionary. In the 1960s this approach broadened with the rise of the theology of development because of the failure of the first strategy.

74. But by the mid-1960s it became clear that the concept of the

development of the underdeveloped was not helpful. It was realized that relations between the West and the Third World were not those of developed vs. underdeveloped, but dominance vs. dependence, oppressor vs. oppressed. It was clear that the gap between rich and poor countries was widening despite, or even because of, the development projects of the 1950s and 1960s. The West had built up a headstart which no evolutionary development projects could overtake. Thus a solution was sought in revolution rather than evolution. The termination of the existing order was demanded, and a completely new beginning called for (Bosch).

This is how the theology of revolution, or the theology of liberation, came into being.

What Revolution Means

75. The word or concept of revolution is used and defined in a number of different ways. The French Revolution let loose a whole set of ideas on the idea of change:
- that the world can change radically and that humanity can break with the past and create a new order;
- that there is a vision of brighter times;
- that the kingdom of the future can be created now.

76. In the philosophy of law, the concept of a revolution is defined as "the seizure of state authority—usually by force—by a person or group with the purpose of bringing about drastic changes in a specific political structure." This rather juridical definition nonetheless leaves open the possibility of a *coup d'état* without the use of violence.

77. Siegmund Neumann defines revolution as a "drastic, fundamental change in the political organization, the social structure; it is a control of the economic domain, and the dominant myth of the social order, which therewith signals a radical break in the continuity of historical development."

78. Social scientists tend to see revolution as a sudden and far-reaching major break in the continuity of development. Pierre Bigo, in his book *The Church and the Third World Revolution* (Orbis: 1977), defines a revolution as a "conscious and intentional change of one society into another society" (p. 6). This is similar to Bosch's view.

79. Karl Rahner, in his article "On the Theology of Revolution"

in *Theological Investigations*, vol. 14 (1976), pp. 320, 324, defines revolution as essentially the recognition of injustices, the conception of new and more just structures, and strategies and methods for change on the part of groups outside the power structure of society.

80. The above conceptualizations indicate that the concept of revolution is widely used to mean different things. My usage in speeches and writings has to do with the concept of radical change as opposed to conservative or liberal models of change. My basis for this conception lies in my understanding of "sin" in theological terms. Confronted with the Gospel of Jesus Christ one has to radically turn away from sin by changing radically from the old sinful nature into a new creature in Christ. There is nothing as radical (or as revolutionary) to me as conversion and reconciliation with God.

81. This is why I cannot understand dealing with apartheid by "reforming" it. This would still leave the core of a heretical system. I believe it has to be transformed, or go through a revolutionary change.

82. Alfredo Fierro argues in his book, *The Militant Gospel* (Orbis: 1977), that revolution attacks the legitimacy and morality of the established order. It seeks to generate new moral presuppositions to break down the prevailing moral order and set up a different morality. The ethics of revolution, he says, decides between the "right of the existing order," and "the right of what might and perhaps should be," on the basis of a "historical calculus" that is rational and basically empirical.

83. In my speeches, for example, I have challenged both the legitimacy of this government, and its morality. It lacks legitimacy because it does not involve the majority of South Africans. It is a minority government, imposing its will on the people without their participation. It lacks morality because it discriminates on the basis of color, race and ethnicity.

84. My moral presupposition is based on my faith, which agrees with the Freedom Charter: that South Africa belongs to all who live in it, both black and white; and that all must participate equally in the government of the country.

85. The revolutionary process of legitimizing the government based on a new morality would begin when Botha's government abandoned apartheid, and sat down with the legitimate leaders of the

people to draft a constitution guaranteeing peace.

86. This process does not need "force" to take place; it needs only those in power to face the reality that they cannot maintain a grossly unjust system for ever.

Revolution over Another Revolution

87. I envisage revolutionary change affecting all facets of society, including both racism and the economy. Revolution thus has to do with structural change. In South Africa, the problem of racism has been used to entrench an apartheid economy which has benefited a minority at the expense of the majority. One cannot talk about change without looking at the inequalities in resources and wealth—for example 87 percent of the land is in the hands of a minority. Change in South Africa has to deal with the question of the redistribution of land, resources and wealth.

88. This has nothing to do with Communism. It has to do with justice. Berryman, in his book *The Religious Roots of Rebellion* (Orbis: 1984), puts it succinctly when he says that "the wealth of the oligarchy is not primarily the result of entrepreneurial genius, but rather the product of an original expropriation and continuing expropriation." In South Africa, this involved the dispossession of the land by the colonialists which still continues in the form of removals and resettlement of people.

89. My concern therefore is not just with the establishment of just government by removing racism, but also establishing economic legitimacy so that the economy serves human needs. A "revolution on top of revolution" indicates that the removal of racism will not resolve all problems. There is also the question of justice in the economy. This is a call for a radical change in the economy to deal with injustices there.

Revolution and Violence

90. In South Africa, the word "revolution" has often been associated with violence. Berryman deals with this general problem, making it clear that he is talking about structural change when he speaks of revolution.

91. It is because of this ambiguity that in those meetings where I spoke of revolution, I attempted to qualify the meaning of the word.

92. However, while adhering to the concept of a peaceful revolution, I also agree with J.F. Kennedy when he said, "Those who make peaceful revolutions impossible will make violent revolutions inevitable."

93. Kennedy's statement makes it clear that there can be both peaceful and violent revolutions, and that the question of violence or otherwise is for rulers to determine.

94. It is for this reason that I prayed for mercy from God that if we continue facing the degree of arrogance from the government on the simple demand for the abolition of apartheid, we are bound to end up with a bloody confrontation.

The Ethics of Means and the Use of Violence

95. There are eight kinds of violence in most oppressive regimes:
1. Institutionalized violence (embedded in the underlying oppressive structures);
2. Repressive state violence (violence to maintain the social system, and in response to counter violence);
3. Right-wing violence;
4. Terrorist violence (which some call revolutionary);
5. Violence of politico-military groups (where they carry out actions that do not aim at innocent victims);
6. Violence of legitimate defense (where a dictatorship seriously offends human rights and the common good of the nation, which becomes unbearable, and channels for dialogue, understanding and rationality are closed). When that happens, the Church speaks of the legitimate right of defense. But the defense must be proportional to the attack;
7. Spontaneous violence (when people are attacked for demanding their rights);
8. The violence of nonviolence (the Gandhi approach: that to be nonviolent is to be divine).

96. Faced with the reality of having no real option for nonviolence in South Africa, one can only opt for different kinds of violence.

The Theology of Revolution

97. In the light of the revolutionary climate in the world today—especially in Latin America—a theology of revolution has devel-

oped. This attempts to ascertain the relationship between the revolutionary activity of human beings, and that of God. It is not a new theological statement, but is a change of perspective which produced new insights into the role of theology in revolution.

98. The Latin American theologians preferred to call their theology "liberation theology," while the European theologians used the phrase "theology of revolution."

99. Liberation theology does not only reflect critically on society, its unjust structures, and the process of bringing about radical change. It also reflects on the life of the Church, analyzing the material structures of the Church and its methods of working in the world.

100. The theology of revolution also implies a revolution in theology, including change in the Church itself.

101. The theology of revolution does not need to be a threat to those in power (state, church, individual) because it has to do with good news to the world, to offer one revolution to end all revolutions. This noble exercise can only threaten those in power who want to maintain injustice.

Songs and Slogans in Meetings

102. During my time as a student at the University of the North (1972–1974), I was first exposed to liberation songs, or what the state has referred to as "revolutionary" or "bellicose" songs.

103. As far as I was concerned, the songs of that time were politically mild, and morally compatible with my Christianity. For example, a song frequently sung then, and now, is *Senzenina*. This is sung as follows:

Senzenina senzenina (four times).

Sono sethu ubumnyama (four times).

This translates as "What have we done, what have we done? Our sin is our blackness."

104. There could be slight variations to this. But when people began to sing the second stanza, *Amabhunu izinja* (Boers are dogs), I always felt uncomfortable, and would stop singing. This expression is dealt with in defense evidence in S vs. Cooper and others (the SASO/BPC trial).

105. Over the years, political struggle has intensified as frustration increased. It became clear that the government was not pre-

pared to abandon apartheid. Particularly after the 1976 shootings, the slogans and songs were radicalized.

106. However, I have not participated in any songs or sloganeering that referred directly to the African National Congress, Umkhonto We Sizwe, arms, or that deal with violence.

107. I have gone out of my way before and after UDF meetings to make it clear that no one should sing or shout slogans that are illegal in South Africa. I and a number of other UDF officials have been involved in this exercise, and at times intervened to stop people singing through the microphone on stage.

108. The difficulty I faced was when songs and slogans came from the audience at meetings. There has never been an easy way of stopping this, and I personally do not believe that any chairperson or speaker could have done so at open public meetings. Many of the youth, in particular, would respond with defiance to such attempts to impose limitations on their activities.

109. The UDF is a front of some 600 organizations with their different traditions, political orientations and perspectives. Officials of the UDF can only advise and caution people about their actions. But because the gambit of agreement between UDF and its affiliates is a limited one, the UDF cannot be held responsible for all activities of its affiliates. This goes for members of affiliates as well.

Symbols and Tradition of Struggle

110. It is widely agreed that the names of Nelson Mandela, Walter Sisulu and their fellow prisoners are well-known both inside and outside South Africa. Whether they were ANC leaders or not, and regardless of whether they took up arms against apartheid, many South Africans see them as authentic leaders. Their stature, history, sacrifices and leadership qualities cannot be challenged, in my view.

111. I have on occasion referred to Mandela and Sisulu in particular as leaders of the people. I still believe this, and see them as one key to justice and peace in South Africa.

112. I do accept that there are other great leaders who have sacrificed much for our struggle—like Chief Albert Luthuli, Robert Sobukwe and Steve Biko. Although they are dead, they remain inspirations. For example, the Soweto Civic Association, a UDF affiliate of which I am a member, has used the name of Luthuli on its banners.

113. I have mentioned the name of Tambo, and perhaps other ANC leaders, in dealing with historical fact and realities that pertain in our struggle. I have also mentioned the PAC and Poqo in some of my writings and speeches, and the name of PAC leader Pokela. I have on occasion made reference to a wide range of other leaders—Machel, Mugabe, Nkomo, Nujoma, Dos Santos, Reagan, Castro and Thatcher. In these cases I refer to such people because they are factors in the South African struggle, whether I like it or not, and regardless of whether I support them and their policies.

Through the Cross: An Interview with Frank Chikane

JIM WALLIS: You're now the General Secretary of the South African Council of Churches, but it was a long road that brought you to this place. Tell us about your background.

FRANK CHIKANE: I grew up in the Apostolic Faith Mission, a conservative, almost fundamentalist, Pentecostal church which later trained me as a pastor. After my ordination, the church began to accuse me of being involved in politics. I had been asked to address a student conference on Christianity and the political situation, and the press picked it up.

The church council produced its file of press cuttings as evidence against me. I still have the letter which says, "You are suspended from pastoral work because you are involved in politics, because you appeared in the press." I was suspended for one year, from 1981 to 1982; I spent eight months of that time in detention.

After my suspension, I joined the Catholic Institute for Contextual Theology, where I spent five and a half years. That experience was very significant. I had started with a very conservative, highly pietistic theology that could justify and accept the status quo; a pastor's job was to prepare people to go to heaven. But then I was confronted by the reality of the oppressive system, which made me raise new questions that were not answered by my training or tradition.

It was extraordinary for me to be appointed general secretary of the Institute for Contextual Theology from the Apostolic Faith Mission. It's even more extraordinary that I was appointed to that position in the South African Council of Churches from that church, which decided in 1975 not to join the Council of Churches. To quote a letter the church circulated after my appointment, the Council of Churches "produces violence and liberation theology to Marxists and Communists."

During my suspension I argued that my church's interpretation of politics is anything that opposed the system. If you do not oppose the system, it's not politics. You can have P. W. Botha addressing you, but you cannot have [Oliver] Tambo [of the African National Congress], because that's politics.

P. W. Botha's letters and the statement from the Dutch Reformed Church are saying exactly the same thing: There is the spiritual realm and the political realm. And if you interfere with the political, you are moving away from what is spiritual and Christian.

But I believe you cannot separate religion from the life experience of people. I do not believe that Jesus Christ came for spiritual human beings rather than concrete human beings who live within a particular historical experience. You have to live your life on that farm or in that township, and your Christianity is tested by how you handle that reality.

Some think you can lead a spiritual life outside your experience. That's why people continue to oppress others. Some Christians don't see anything wrong in exploiting farm workers, because that is not spirituality, and they can still go to church on Sunday and do their spiritual thing.

So your conservative evangelical background did provide you, as mine provided me, a faith and a biblical foundation that you use against the system now.
I don't regret growing up in the Apostolic Faith Mission because the church has a particular quality of spirituality which helps you to survive. When I sat in the jail cell, I needed to refer back to that spirituality. I needed to say that there is something more than the life I am living here.

I had to be able to say to the guy who tortured me—who happened to be a deacon of my church in the white congregation—
"For me, to live is Christ, to die is gain. If you kill me, I go to heaven, and it doesn't solve your problem. But if you release me, then I continue preaching the gospel. It does not matter which way you take it, because both ways you're going to be a loser."

They said to me, "You're going to die slowly but surely. Why not decide quickly what you want to do?"

And I said to them, "Well, you also have to make your decision because I'm not going to change my mind. If you put me under pressure hoping to change my mind, I might die, you see. And you might not have planned to kill me. So you need to make your decision whether in fact you want to kill me or not."

You could easily be suicidal when you are subjected to torture. The torturers actually say, "Why not commit suicide, because you're going to die in a terrible way."

And I said, "No, I'm not going to deprive you of the responsibility of my death."

When you sit in that jail cell, you realize you aren't in control of the world. And that spirituality, that sense of your own limits and dependence on the Lord, which could be seen as a traditional theological position, is very helpful. And that's why I've kept my membership with the church. And I worship there every Sunday.

How often have you been detained and under what circumstances?
I've been detained five times since 1977. The first one was in January 1977 for seven days. Within an hour after my detention, I couldn't walk. They used brutal third-degree methods of torture.

And then I was detained again from June 1977 until January 1978, and I went through six weeks of torture. It was during that detention that the deacon of my church in the white congregation supervised the fifty-hour period where I was interrogated around-the-clock. During the forty-eighth hour, when I realized the torture was affecting my mental state, I told him, "I'm not going to answer any more questions. You can do what you want to." And they tried for two more hours and then got me out of the chains and dropped me in solitary confinement where they ignored me for six months.

But that deacon simply believed that he was doing his work. He knows I'm the pastor of a church. But he believes he's stopping the communists and the terrorists of this country. Whites in this country are worried about a Marxist takeover; we are worried about a Christian government which oppresses other Christians.

In 1980 I was detained for a short moment simply because P. W. Botha was coming to the area. The longest detention was from 1981 to 1982. Then during the 1985 UDF [United Democratic Front] treason trial, I was detained for two and a half months.

It seems the role of the church has changed a good deal since your ordination.
The missionary church—the main channel of the church in South Africa—consisted of European or American missionaries who were on the side of the colonizers and therefore couldn't see the evils of the system. At worst, they directly supported the system; at best, they took a liberal position of saying, "Don't be excessive if you oppress them."

In the '60s, when [ANC leader Nelson] Mandela was sentenced to prison, other people were jailed, and organizations banned, the churches supported the government.

But then in the '70s, the Black Consciousness Movement came into the picture. More and more black people took up leadership roles. By 1975 the shade of the Council of Churches was shifting completely, with more black presence. And now it is a true reflection of the population distribution in the country—it is 80 percent black.

Now the church is beginning to reflect critically on the reality of the situation, and it is able to take a prophetic position. You don't often find a church or church structure—particularly an ecumenical structure—declaring a government illegitimate. But the South African Council of Churches last year declared this government illegitimate and said that we are not obliged to obey these unjust laws.

The conditions in the country—the level of brutality, the pain and suffering that ordinary church people see—move them to think in a more critical way about the system and become more determined to remove it. February 24 of this year [the effective banning of opposition organizations] was a historic event because it got the church leaders to take a stand that has never been taken before.

The government created a crisis of the churches. The churches had been talking about nonviolence and peaceful change, and most of them had condemned violence. But now the church leaders felt we could no longer just talk about nonviolence; we needed to act. So we marched in Cape Town.

We have proved that today the road of nonviolence in South Africa is very short. The system doesn't allow for nonviolent activity. I interpreted the government order of February 24 as saying to the victims of apartheid, "We can't handle you at the nonviolent political level, so we're closing all the doors; we want you at the military level."

Interestingly, Adrian Vlok, the minister of law and order, said in Parliament, "These organizations realized that they couldn't match us at the military level. That's why they opted for what they call 'nonviolent mobilization of the masses' to create a revolutionary situation." South Africa, in essence, opted for violence on the 24th of February. That's what created the crisis for the church leaders. So you needed to be honest enough to go and march.

I've talked about honest and dishonest nonviolent disciples. Dishonest nonviolent disciples raise nonviolence to stop people from resisting the system. But honest nonviolent disciples want to see nonviolent protest working.

I was a bit worried when the decision was made on Thursday, February 25, for us to march; I felt that this could divide the Council of Churches. Now you can imagine what that means to the General Secretary. But amazingly, the brutal act of the state united the church leaders and caused us to make a decision to do something we could never do before. We came out of the march more united than ever. I think we are going to broaden the ecumenical structure in South Africa more than white people ever thought.

Since the march, the air is full of accusations from the government against the churches. You have been at the center of much of this because of your letter to P. W. Botha and his now-famous letter in response, which attacked the church leaders.

I suspect that the state is going to be forced to be more brutal against the church simply because of the amazing determination of church leaders. I suspect that the state might try other than just the legal methods of dealing with church leaders. We are already experiencing harassment and attacks. We might have to go through an experience of assassinations and people disappearing. I believe that the state is going to try to close this space for the church.

The state is saying the church leaders are not really church leaders, that the people will not follow them.
I don't think the state president has the credentials to decide whether we are church or not. They [government leaders] are used to the Dutch Reformed Church, which blesses the state, so when you begin to question them, they say, "You are not the church."

You could see from the upsurge of support for the church leaders that we are planning to get the body of Christ—the whole body, the congregations—taking up the issues themselves. I find it amazing that the churches in South Africa—at least those who are member churches of the Council—have moved away from debate about whether they can or should do anything as a church. They are debating what type of action they need to take.

The attacks on the church by the state have, in fact, mobilized more Christians. This mobilization that P.W. has caused is amazing. The government will have to face a massive upsurge of the members of the churches against the apartheid system. Anything they do besides going to the negotiating table is going to make the situation worse.

What will happen when honest, nonviolent disciples take their place in the streets, willing to put their lives on the line against a system that has demonstrated its willingness to be so vicious and brutal? What is ahead for the church and the country in this period?
I think we are going through the worst period, and it's going to become much worse than it is at the present moment. I suspect that as the congregations go to the streets, the system is going to be more and more brutal. And it's going to mean the murder of a lot of our people. And in the course of the murder of our people, the system will begin to disintegrate because of the contradictions created by its own brutality.

It seems—and this is a painful thing—that the international community does not respond unless we die in great numbers. When we want to take on the system, some say, "You're committing suicide, you know. You're going to be murdered." And we say, "Can you help us?" If they say, "No, we cannot help you," what they are telling us is to leave the system to oppress us indefinitely. So we find ourselves in a vulnerable situation where we cannot do otherwise but, in fact, offer ourselves for sacrifice.

I don't believe we can avoid the cross as a church now. If Jesus Christ had an option, I would think he also would not have gone to the cross. One theologian said, "Jesus Christ didn't choose to die. He simply had no option but to die."

And it looks as though we have no option in the face of the level of evil in this country. For us to go over into victory, we will have to go through the cross.

Through that experience of the cross, I believe the system is going to be put down, and the church will come out being the real church of Christ. In this situation, if you're not a persecuted church, it seems that you can't become a real church of Christ.

Now we are faced with the reality that to be a Christian has to be a conscious decision. It is going to be too costly for those who became Christians by tradition or chance. Some might withdraw from the church. People will have to make very conscious decisions, knowing that to choose Christ is to choose death for the sake of justice against evil.

By going through that experience, we are forced to review our Christian faith, our own commitment. And that might be helpful in cleansing the church in South Africa. But I'm convinced that our victory is going to be at the level of that experience.

What can you say about the role of whites in this struggle?
A small number of whites have taken a stand against the apartheid system. And their presence in our midst helps us to lessen the type of pain people go through. If we could get many white Christians to come in, it would help to lessen the pain even more.

But I'm not very hopeful that this will happen. Those churches with whites in them would have to begin to preach the gospel in such a way that whites would have to choose whether they would stay in those churches. At the end we would have church members who would take a stand against the government which gives them the benefits.

Your situation seems to many on the outside to be hopeless. Yet I'm deeply amazed and moved, as you face the cross, by the hope that you and others express again and again.

I think one feels pessimistic when one approaches the problem from a pastoral perspective. As a pastor you're concerned about the lives of people, the pain they are going to go through. You wish that it wouldn't happen. It is just like Jesus saying, "I wish that this cup would pass." Humanly no one wants to go through that experience.

But on the other hand, it is that experience that gives you hope, because through that experience one has redemption, one has freedom. And because there's no option, we're bound as Christians to go through that experience.

Especially during 1986, as the system became more brutal, the young people said they actually felt they were closer to their liberation. They understand the fact that you cannot get closer to liberation without bringing out the viciousness of the system. The pain is an indication of the closeness to your day of liberation.

It is our faith that gives us hope. We know that in our helplessness we become more dependent on God. In our powerlessness we become powerful. It is our weakness that is our strength.

Those who run the evil system know it will end, and therefore they have no hope. They just become madder by the day, and in their madness take more and more lives.

But we know that our struggle is a just one. That is really what makes it hopeful—God cannot allow evil to prevail forever.

One would hope that as you move toward the cross, the eyes and ears and hearts of the church all over the world would be awakened to respond.

Our act is redemptive—not in the sense that Christ died to redeem the world—but that, in our weakness, our experience helps other people to have a new understanding of their faith and their commitment. And so the suffering of the church in South Africa itself becomes a message of salvation and hope and redemption for the greater body of Christ.

CPSIA information can be obtained
at www.ICGtesting.com
Printed in the USA
LVHW081612101219
640064LV00037B/1272/P